TELL THE TRUTH AND SHAME THE DEVIL

TELL THE TRUTH AND SHAME THE DEVIL

FOR NEARLY 20 YEARS ALAN MORRIS ABUSED
BOYS AT MY SCHOOL. DECADES LATER THE
EX-PUPILS REUNITED AND BROUGHT HIM
TO JUSTICE. THIS IS HOW WE DID IT.

DAVID NOLAN

JOHN BLAKE

Published by John Blake Publishing Ltd,
3 Bramber Court, 2 Bramber Road,
London W14 9PB, England

www.johnblakebooks.com

www.facebook.com/johnblakebooks ⓕ
twitter.com/jblakebooks ⓔ

This edition published in paperback in 2015

ISBN: 978 1 78418 422 3

British Library Cataloguing-in-Publication Data:

A catalogue record for this book is available from the British Library.

Design by www.envydesign.co.uk

Printed in Great Britain by CPI Group (UK) Ltd

1 3 5 7 9 10 8 6 4 2

Papers used by John Blake Publishing are natural, recyclable products
made from wood grown in sustainable forests. The manufacturing processes
conform to the environmental regulations of the country of origin.

Every attempt has been made to contact the relevant copyright-holders,
but some were unobtainable. We would be grateful if the appropriate people
could contact us.

ABOUT THE AUTHOR

David Nolan has been a journalist since the day he left school in 1981. He has worked for newspapers and magazines, in radio and television, and has won multiple Royal Television Society awards for his documentaries and current-affairs programmes. This is his tenth book.

For the lads...

CONTENTS

ACKNOWLEDGEMENTS

Journalists are always late to the party. Always. We arrive once the riot is coming to an end, an hour after the shooting has occurred, or as the dust is settling once the bomb has gone off.

But in the case of Alan Morris and St Ambrose College, I was very much there – although I really would have preferred to be somewhere else. I was there when the beatings were dished out at our Christian Brothers school in the leafy village of Hale Barns, south of Manchester. I was there when Morris used corporal punishment as a way of satisfying his sexual desires. Indeed, he did it to me as he did to so many others.

So it's with thanks to Greater Manchester Police officers DI Jed Pidd, DC Barry Conway and DC Nicola Graham that I was also able to be there thirty-five years later, during Morris's historical sex-abuse trial. I was there when evidence boxes were loaded into the car on the first day of the trial; I was there when he arrived at court – in fact, I earned myself a reprimand from the judge for confronting my old chemistry teacher – and I was there when Alan Morris was sentenced for his crimes.

I was holding DC Graham's hand when the sentence was read out, or perhaps I should say she was holding mine. It was Nicola who first said to me, 'You're an author, David, you should write a book about this case...'

Many other people have helped to tell this story: Helen Tonge, Ian Bradshaw and Laura Robinson from Title Role Productions; Lucy West and Ashley Derricott from Granada Television; Charlotte Crangle from the Crown Prosecution Service; Paul Malpas; Ken and Margaret Nolan; Elsie Mitchell; Mollie Whittall and Richard Scorer from Slater & Gordon and John Kennedy of the St Ambrose Old Boys' Association. Thanks also to Chris Mitchell at John Blake Publishing and to Paul Woods.

Crucially, many St Ambrose pupils from different eras stepped up to tell their tale, so I give huge thanks to Mike Bishop, Richard Eames, Tim Gresty, David Lee, Scott Morgan, Simon O'Brien, David Prior, Paul Quinn, Andy Rothwell, Derek Scanlan, Neil Summers and Paul Wills, along with those ex-pupils, parents and others who cannot be named: 'Ground Zero Boy', 'Nervous Boy', 'Doctor Boy', 'Doctor Dad', 'Gallery Boy', 'Police Boy', 'Business Boy' and 'Investigation Woman'. You know who you are but I respect the fact that you don't want other people to know.

I never thought I'd have anything to do with St Ambrose

after I left in 1981 and no one is more surprised than I am that this book even exists. As an adult, I'd sometimes tell people how tough the school was but, like many other ex-pupils, I never really spoke about how dark things actually were. We boxed it up and hid it away.

Thanks to the ex-pupils who have come forward all those individual boxes have now been opened. Through their brave actions, other people may now learn from what happened.

That's about as close as we're likely to get in terms of something 'good' coming out of this. The rest of it stinks...

David Nolan, Manchester 2015
@davidnolanwriter

All photos, unless otherwise stated, are by Katherine Macfarlane: www.shesnaps.com

INTRODUCTION

'NO ONE HEALS HIMSELF BY
WOUNDING ANOTHER.' –
ST AMBROSE OF MILAN

We were used to Mr Morris – chemistry teacher at St Ambrose College – being in a fury but this was off the scale. He swept into the laboratory late that day – this hyper-organised teacher was normally early – and slammed the stack of books and folders he was carrying onto the front desk where the first row of boys sat. I was in the back row; I wasn't a front-row kind of pupil.

There was a long silence.

'Someone... has been talking about me,' he said, pacing up and down in front of us. 'Someone... has been telling stories about me.'

As the pacing continued he balled his hands into fists, holding them tightly by his side. He looked like a caricature of a 1970s chemistry teacher: wavy, side-parted black hair; spectacles; a brown jacket with leather patches on the elbows.

The pacing continued. 'Someone... has been telling lies about me.' The pacing stopped. 'If any boy were to say anything about me, tell stories about me, tell lies about me, I would leave this school.' Morris paused and brought his right fist level with his face. 'But I would take the teeth of the boy who said it with me.'

This was followed by a really long silence. Then the lesson began.

It was 1978 and I was thirteen years old. But it would be nearly twenty-five years until anyone plucked up the courage to say anything about Alan Morris outside the school grounds; then a further ten years until that ex-pupil was believed and dozens more boys would come forward. Only they were no longer boys by this stage; they were middle-aged men and the stories they told would put Morris behind bars.

They would tell the police of ritualised beatings, sexual assaults and acts of gross indecency carried out under the guise of corporal punishment. Older 'boys' would also come forward, telling of sex attacks at the hands of teachers who worked alongside Morris at St Ambrose; attacks that they had stayed silent about for decades.

It all stayed hidden until Greater Manchester Police launched their biggest historical sex-abuse investigation thus far, to get to the truth behind what happened to all those boys so many years ago.

Indeed, truth had been a very important facet of life at our Catholic school. The motto of St Ambrose remains to this day '*Vitam Impendere Vero*': 'Life Depends on Truth.' It's on the badge of every boy's blazer.

But there was an unofficial motto that some teachers would quote as they doled out terrible beatings that stayed with the pupils for the rest of their lives. It would come back to haunt Alan Morris, the Christian Brothers and other staff from St Ambrose College with its direct quote from Shakespeare's *Henry IV, Part 1*: 'Tell the truth and shame the Devil!' They'd say it just before they hit you.

This is the story of how the truth would finally be told and the Devil eventually shamed.

CHAPTER ONE

THE DEVIL AT
THE ALTAR

It's 2001 and the phone rings at the Holy Angels Roman Catholic Church, Hale Barns, on the comfy southern edge of Greater Manchester. The man making the call wants to speak to Deacon Alan Morris. There's a lot going on in the tone of his voice: calm and clear but also insistent, angry and upset – as he has good reason to be. For he's just been told by officers from Greater Manchester Police that 'no further action' is going to be taken regarding a complaint about Deacon Morris. And it's a very serious complaint indeed.

It has taken the man on the phone more than twenty years to build up the courage to tell the police something he's never told anyone before: that Deacon Morris had repeatedly beaten and sexually assaulted him over a three-year period when he was a boy.

1

Back then, Morris had been a chemistry teacher at St Ambrose College, the prestigious boys' school next door to the church. The man making the call had been his pupil and he was the first person to tell police about Alan Morris.

Let's call him Ground Zero Boy.

By 2001 he was in his mid-thirties but the memories of what happened to him were still fresh in his mind and raw in his heart.

'Imagine sending your lad to school, in his shiny new uniform and his new sports bag,' Ground Zero told me, trying to put into words how it felt to have those memories raked over again. 'You give him all the guidance about what's right and what's wrong, how to be a good person, a good guy. You watch him walk up the school path and get smaller and smaller and disappear into the milieu. Then years later you find out he ended up in a lonely room, on his own with Alan Morris. Imagine that's tomorrow morning. It doesn't bear thinking about. You'd feel you'd want to destroy that situation; destroy that possibility. I'm glad to say that for some years to come – though not enough – we've succeeded in stopping Alan Morris.'

But on that day in 2001 it was a long way in the future. Morris seemed out of reach and an opportunity had been missed. Ground Zero Boy was informed that, despite pouring his heart out to officers about what had happened to him, they'd spoken to Deacon Morris and decided not to pursue the matter any further; the Deacon was free to return to his work at Holy Angels.

'I'm sure that, having found the courage to come forward,

that person must have felt extremely let down,' says Detective Inspector Jed Pidd, the detective who would head the new investigation into Morris in 2012. 'I can only apologise for that. Both the strength and the weakness of the system is that there's a certain level of proof needed – a threshold of evidence that we have to adhere to – that ensures there aren't miscarriages of justice.'

But a miscarriage of justice is exactly what Ground Zero Boy felt was occurring – which was why he decided to ring Holy Angels. He wanted Deacon Alan Morris to admit to what he'd done; to confirm what had happened in a storage space behind the St Ambrose chemistry lab, known as 'the Dark Room'; he wanted him to confess.

So he got Morris on the phone but the Deacon was having none of it. It was then that, despite living on the south coast of England, Ground Zero decided to get in his car and drive 300 miles to Hale Barns, to confront Morris face to face; whatever it took to break the malign will of his ex-teacher.

'I wanted him to look me in the eye and say, "Yeah, I did it,"' Ground Zero told the jury at Alan Morris's trial in 2014. 'Say you did it. That'll do for me.'

What followed was an extraordinary game of telephonic cat and mouse between the two men as Ground Zero travelled north. He repeatedly rang his former teacher and tried to extract a confession – while Deacon Morris did everything in his power to avoid giving one.

However, he did tell Ground Zero that he'd thought about killing himself, as had his own brother – whereas, in fact, Alan Morris's brother was very much alive. He also admitted he had 'committed many sins against many people' but still Ground Zero wasn't hearing what he wanted to hear.

Eventually, as his pursuer got closer, reaching the outskirts of Birmingham, Alan Morris – Deacon of the Holy Angels Roman Catholic Church, the man who would later be dubbed 'the Dirty Dean of Discipline' in court – said the desired word when asked, 'Did you do it?'

'Yes,' whispered Morris.

The line went quiet.

'Well, I've forgiven you,' Ground Zero said. 'So don't kill yourself.'

He hung up, turned his car around and headed home.

Alan Morris is now in jail for what he did to Ground Zero and other boys at St Ambrose. There would be so much evidence against him that it was spread across three separate trials, to avoid confusing a single jury with the sheer volume of testimony. At the end of legal proceedings, Judge Timothy Mort described Morris's perverted reign over the school as a 'shocking abuse of trust'. Detectives investigating the attacks described them as occurring on an 'industrial scale'.

But in the course of bringing Morris to justice, police based at the Public Protection Unit at Altrincham, Greater Manchester, discovered an even darker heart to the story – claims that Morris had not been the only one to abuse boys at the school.

'Having investigated St Ambrose, I believe there were people there who had offended for years prior to Alan Morris,' DI Pidd of GMP told me. 'Those people carried out really horrendous acts of sexual abuse against those young children.'

The 2010s has been the decade in which the concept of 'historical abuse' has really hit home. It's no longer just part of the terminology of criminologists and psychologists but a parade of grim incidents and hurtful memories that have entered the culture via a dark series of notorious cases – none more so than that of Jimmy Savile.

We see the crowing headlines when the cases result in a prosecution and hear the screams for heads to roll when they do not. We also hear declamatory howls of 'How was it allowed to happen?' and witness the collective handwringing as we're promised 'lessons will be learned' from the whole experience.

Then the whole cycle repeats itself with a familiarity that would be tiresome if it wasn't so infuriating.

So where does this clamour for justice to be done over offences committed decades ago come from? What actually happens if you come forward to make a complaint of historical abuse? How do the police investigate such crimes? Perhaps if we could see inside the process, hear from those involved and understand what actually happens, maybe we'd have a clearer view and be able to dispel a few myths.

So let's try and do just that. Let's lay a case out from beginning to end, starting at the institution that allowed it to happen and ending with the repercussions for all those involved. Let's do it from the very heart of the investigation into St Ambrose College.

The key perpetrator in the St Ambrose case was obviously

Alan Morris himself. Detective Constable Nicola Graham, who helped take the case through court, described to me the man and his methodology:

'He picked on vulnerable children to give them corporal punishment in an environment where he could do it without anyone else seeing,' she told me. 'While punishing them, he sexually abused them. He was a very powerful man and he was very scary. He had a big audience to choose from. To him, the school was like a sweetshop.'

The Morris case also demonstrates how many of the assumptions and clichés associated with historical cases don't necessarily apply. There were no care-home victims here; no street urchins from broken homes; no lack of worldliness or intelligence on the part of the victims or their parents. These were 'nice' kids from 'good' families.

Throughout the investigation, detectives would comment on how highly educated the victims were and how articulately they expressed themselves. When it came to the trial, the witness box was visited by doctors, businessmen, journalists, consultants... even a headmaster. Many of 'the lads' – as all the ex-pupils tend to refer to themselves – had done well in life.

They didn't need to be at Minshull Street Crown Court in Manchester in that baking-hot summer of 2014. But they felt the need to tell the truth. If the Devil would be shamed in the process, so be it.

But still, the men who came forward to testify against Morris had been tethered to their past for decades. It had never left them, though some had travelled far and wide to get away from it. Distance may have numbed it, muffled its background noise, but it couldn't silence its constant hum. At least one of Morris's victims tried to kill himself after leaving the school.

Another victim who gave evidence told me his reaction on seeing Morris again, years after he'd left the school. He'd gone travelling in Australia and had been away for a long time. In the meantime, Morris had become a deacon at the church right next door to St Ambrose.

'I went into Holy Angels for a funeral and I saw him on the altar, standing next to the priest in his vestments,' the ex-pupil told me. 'I didn't know what a panic attack was but I know what they are now. I remember running outside, I think I was trying to be sick and I just thought, *Oh God... I can't believe it. I think I've just seen the Devil at the altar!*'

The Alan Morris case shows that abuse can happen to anyone, whatever their background. It just needs enough people to turn a blind eye and inaction on the part of adults whose job it is look after those too young to fully look after themselves. It thrives in situations where people are afraid of upsetting the status quo, scared of 'what people might say'. It loves it when adults and children are afraid of authority, or even of someone they themselves have empowered.

For this is all about power. Alan Morris wielded power over pupils, parents and his colleagues – and no one stood up to him. As DI Jed Pidd says,

'I've got no doubt that, in certain respects and in relation to certain pupils, he was an excellent teacher. But all of that was imbued with a degree and level of control that he exercised over individuals and the school as a whole that was very unhealthy – because it was unchallenged and it was unmet.'

No one challenged Morris as he took boys into the Dark Room behind his chemistry lab; no one queried how his administration of corporal punishment was turned into a long, theatrical extravaganza; his use of disciplinary beatings as an excuse to molest boys went unmet. The pupils at St Ambrose College were afraid of him – but so, too, it appears were the other members of staff. *Everyone* was fearful of Alan Morris.

'The lads knew to stay away from him, stay out of the chemistry lab, stay out of the room behind the lab,' another ex-pupil and trial witness told me. 'It wasn't about the thrashings, it was about the intense sense of fear that you felt when you walked into that lab or that back room. It was about vulnerability, it was about the anticipation of what might happen next... basically, sexual violence. None of the lads were scared about taking a battering, that was OK. It was about the anticipation of sexual violence and the way he prolonged it – it was like a horror movie really. When you're waiting for that moment... it strikes fear into your heart. And because we were young, we felt very vulnerable.'

If anyone should have been in a position to empathise with kids who felt vulnerable, it should have been Alan Richard Morris. He was brought up with a series of challenges that marked him out as different to other boys. 'I had an extremely difficult childhood,' he later told the police during hours of interviews after his arrest. 'Quite exceptionally unhappy.'

Born on 6 November 1949 into what was later described as 'difficult financial circumstances', he contracted polio as a child, leaving him with one leg shorter than the other and requiring him to wear a built-up shoe. Morris's mother was disabled too, while his brother Kevin suffered from debilitating depression and social alienation. Kevin would never work and it would be down to Alan to go out into the world and make something of himself. Despite this, Alan would often describe his brother Kevin as 'the clever one'.

Despite being born some distance from the pole position in life, Alan was a bright lad too. He went to Altrincham Grammar School, not far from his home in Hale, between 1961 and 1968. He excelled there – although he did manage to get on the wrong side of the chemistry teacher at the school, earning some beatings with a Bunsen burner tube. The stiff, rubber hose was the weapon of choice for chemistry teachers at the time and being beaten with it was clearly something that stayed with the young Alan.

From the age of seventeen, Morris was, in his own words, a 'discreet homosexual'; this realisation came just before he left Hale to go to university. He went to Queens College, Cambridge, to study natural science, specialising in chemistry. His mother must have been very proud. Afterwards, he returned north for a post-graduate course at Manchester University.

Morris had a flamboyant, theatrical air and had toyed with the idea of becoming an actor, although teaching was his preferred choice for a future career. Having decided that his future lay in education, he took a six-week placement at a school in Wythenshawe. Though geographically close to Hale and Altrincham, Wythenshawe was socially a world away. At the time it was the biggest council estate in Europe and the toughness of both the regime and the pupils must have been a shock for a grammar school lad like Alan.

He would later recall hearing what he thought was a hearty round of applause on entering the school on his first day; it was, in fact, the sound of scores of lads, all in a line, being 'strapped' – beaten on the hand with a long, multi-layered strip of leather. The strap was a standard piece of kit in British state schools until corporal punishment was made illegal in 1987. Until it was outlawed, it was supposedly guided by two principles: it had to be proportionate and it had to be reasonable.

When, at the end of his placement, Morris got his first proper job at St Ambrose in Hale Barns, he must have thought he'd fallen on his feet. Here was a school with a constituency of pupils from much better-off families than the Wythenshawe crowd but with an equal opportunity for the infliction of corporal punishment.

St Ambrose has occupied its prominent, tree-lined position alongside Hale Road in Hale Barns since 1946. It's a Christian Brothers' school – for the uninitiated, the brothers look, dress and, in some ways, act like priests but have no powers of sacrament; they cannot give the marriage rites, hear confession or give communion.

The order was founded by Edmund Rice in Ireland at the turn of the nineteenth century to help poor kids in Waterford (in the southeast of the Emerald Isle) get an education. The movement spread to England via Liverpool and beyond.

What many boys would experience was essentially a tough Waterford education, transplanted to mainland Britain.

'The Irish Christian Brothers came from an agricultural environment,' recalls ex-pupil Tim Gresty, who started at St Ambrose in 1953. 'And if a horse misbehaves in that environment, you don't talk to it and give it a carrot, you belt it with a big stick.'

The Christian Bothers arrived in the south Manchester area after evacuation from Guernsey in the Channel Islands in 1940, using temporary sites in and around Hale and Altrincham to run schools during the Second World War. The brothers were initially from the De La Salle Order – a slightly more benign proposition than their counterpart Edmund Rice, whose order took over the school after their predecessors returned to the Channel Islands after the war.

During the De La Salle order's tenure, they managed to buy a substantial home called Woodeaves, which came with twenty-two acres of woodland and park, between Whicker Lane and Hale Road. The Brothers moved in on Christmas Eve 1945. Woodeaves would serve as both classroom and accommodation for the school for more than fifteen years.

'My first impression of Woodeaves was a very ornate front door, a beautifully fitted little chapel and lots of small rooms which were the classrooms,' Tim Gresty told me. 'There was a long wooden temporary building that looked like something out of an army camp as well and we used to drop compasses through the holes in the floor to try to hit the rats. It was very basic and rural and primitive but we got tremendous care and support from the staff, nearly all of whom were Irish Christian

Brothers. I remember them all in black like crows, smoking their cigarettes. There were a small number of lay masters, male and female. You could have got all the pupils onto a decent-sized double-decker bus. There was gruff discipline there too. It's what we thought posh schools did. There was very much a feeling of, *We're a cut above the run-of-the-mill day schools in the area. We're something special.*'

By the mid-1950s the school was becoming a victim of its own success; it underwent a small-scale expansion by adding prefab buildings. This still didn't provide enough space, so it was decided to launch a fundraising campaign to bring the school up to date.

'The old place was a bit of a dump but we didn't know any different,' says Tim, whose mother was a leading light among parent fundraisers. 'There was a realisation that these old-style schools that were like day private schools were dying. When I was fourteen or fifteen, I saw these plans for the new building and then this school started to grow next to us. It was extraordinary. It opened in 1963. We had these wonderful facilities. It was stunning. It was awesome. The Christian Brothers were hugely proud of it because it was a modern school, rather than a patched-up bombsite with old Nissan huts. There was huge pride in this modern, slick building. Thinking back, it was probably a bit crude and basic and scruffy – but, to us, it was amazing. We could all eat at the same time and there were speech days, rugby teams, choirs and events.'

Gresty recalls being a pupil in the very first class to use the new school's chemistry lab – the one later used by Alan Morris.

For many years, church services for the boys were held at the chapel at Woodeaves, before it was decided to raise funds for a church to accompany the new school. St Ambrose and Holy Angels Church would be inextricably linked from that moment onwards, eventually sitting side by side.

I asked Tim Gresty if there was anything about St Ambrose during his years, either at Woodeaves or at the new school, which could have contributed to the regime of abuse that was to come.

'The teaching was very good but rigorous,' he told me. 'We knew nothing else. The punishment levels were severe but always publicly done in front of the class, usually with the strap or occasionally with a cricket wicket. It was hard and stern. It was fair but I don't remember any favourites in the class. I was academically well up but I got blasted just as much as anyone. I was a bit lippy and cheeky. In retrospect, I do think that the policy of immediate and slightly demeaning physical punishment created an environment where people would think that was the norm. I think, with that, there's less of a respect for the individual. We were all equal. I wonder if the disciplinary behaviour of the Irish Christian Brothers created an environment where other people coming into it, in positions of responsibility, could think it was not only normal but a reasonable starting point. Therefore, to increase the quality of the discipline, you had to increase the seriousness, the nastiness and the horror of the punishment. That may be a long-term result.'

The strap (some brothers used barbers' strops to hit boys with), the cane and the slipper were standard fare at the school. When biology and drama teacher Norman Wilkinson – known to staff and pupils as 'Sam' – arrived at the school in the late 1960s, he introduced a new and typically theatrical weapon to the armoury: a sawn-off cricket bat known as 'Wilbur the Bottom Slayer'. It had been cut in two so that Wilkinson could transport it in his briefcase. One strike on the backside with Wilbur was enough for any boy. The child had to autograph it afterwards – by the time I arrived at the school, it was black with ink.

Wilkinson managed to charm several generations of boys at the school. His job teaching biology seemed to be a side issue compared to his preferred task of running the school's stage staff (including fully-functioning wardrobe and props departments) and mounting ambitious theatrical productions.

Drama was the one thing St Ambrose seemed to excel at and Wilkinson provided plenty of his own: showing porn in his biology lessons; demonstrating his party trick of independently wiggling either of his ears; slipping favoured lads tins of beer at opportune moments – sometimes allowing them to hide the tins on the shelves under their desks during lessons. Wilkinson was also a keen filmmaker and would encourage lads and their families to take part in his productions.

'He asked me during my GCSEs,' remembers ex-pupil and trial witness Andy Rothwell. 'All year he was buttering me up: "You're a tall lad, a good looking lad, I'm doing a film round my house. I want you to come round during the summer so I can film you. You'll be wearing an old school uniform, shorts, long socks and a cap." I told my dad – he wouldn't let me go.'

Filming boys in period costume that involved shorts

(particularly lederhosen) was a popular pastime for Wilkinson. I appeared in one of his films dressed as a ghostly sailor boy in white shorts – my dad was in it too. I never saw the finished product, as a mysterious technical problem meant it never saw the light of day.

Alan Morris – who'd form a lasting friendship with Wilkinson – arrived at the school in 1972 under the head-mastership of Brother Gleason, who stepped down a year later. The new head, Brother Ring, clearly took a shine to Morris; it's possible that they bonded over their shared love of classical music as the two would go to concerts together, particularly by Manchester's famous Hallé Orchestra.

Despite this, Morris was well down the pecking order of the school. He'd later recall how his briefcase was essentially his office during his first years at St Ambrose. But he rolled up his sleeves and got involved in school life, taking a group of sixth-formers on a trip to Quarr Abbey on the Isle of Wight, to experience the lives of Benedictine monks and listen to their haunting Gregorian chants.

Students took to teasing the new teacher by peppering him with detailed questions about local churches when they went out on tours. It was only later that Morris discovered the lads had revised every church beforehand from guide books, ensuring they knew more about them than their new teacher did. They presented him with the book at the end of the first trip.

Almost immediately, Morris started using corporal punish-ment as a form of sexual assault. He later freely admitted that he preferred to hit boys on the backside, rather than their hands, because it was 'less painful' for them. Morris claimed that he found the preferred instrument at St Ambrose – the leather strap – to be 'positively vicious' and 'couldn't bring myself' to use it. He initially used his open palm on the backside of lads who misbehaved, with the boys leaned facedown over his lap.

Morris would later claim he felt there was no point in beating boys over poor work, only over matters of discipline. Over the years, he would alter the weapon of choice that he used on boys and experimented with different implements: he tried the slipper, a hefty training shoe – 'not my favourite', he later said; then there was a 12-inch ruler, a wooden spoon and even a device of his own invention, a flesh-coloured leather paddle known as the 'Paddywhack'. He also experimented with the Bunsen burner tube – the very device he'd been hit with at school – but claimed it was too uncontrollable, having hurt himself while whacking it on the chemistry lab desk and abandoning it as a means of punishment.

But victim testimony during his trial would show this to be a lie. More than thirty years after Morris started at the school, one ex-pupil came forward to tell police how Morris beat him with the tubing and sexually assaulted him nearly every week over a two-year period starting in 1972. The boy, aged twelve at the time, was taken into the Dark Room after being picked on for 'no apparent reason'. He was told to take down his trousers and pants and was beaten on the bare buttocks half a dozen times. Morris would also touch the boy's genitals.

By the following year, the boy could stand it no longer. When Morris picked on him once again, he stormed out of the class and went to speak to Brother Gleason, who was headmaster at the time. The boy was ignored. This is the first known occurrence of someone speaking out about sexualised beatings at the hands of Alan Morris. It's also the first noted occasion that nothing was done about it.

It set a pattern that would continue for the best part of twenty years: corporal punishment was the excuse that Morris used to isolate a boy from his peers, beat him and molest him. So what did St Ambrose College do about this man who so clearly enjoyed beating young boys? They made him head of discipline in the early 1980s.

Other teachers would delegate punishments to him; an already terrifying figure was given the power to do as he pleased. The sense of fear that he instilled in the boys was a vital element in the pleasure he took and Morris would ramp up the fear factor considerably as the years went by. The greater the terror he could create, the more humiliated the pupil would feel, the more Morris enjoyed it and the less likely the boy was to speak of it. It was a perfect circle.

Morris's enthusiasm for corporal punishment in many ways matched the ongoing levels of violence across the school, designed to inflict pain and humiliation. Ground Zero Boy and several other ex-pupils described to me how they were forced to kneel down and lean forward with a stick of chalk between their teeth and their hands behind their backs. Soon their bodies would be shaking, legs wracked with pain and uniforms covered in saliva and chalk dust.

'It was a violent place,' Ground Zero told me, sharing memories of the school he started at in 1976. 'These days it wouldn't last five seconds. I was beaten with everything you could think of. We were tortured. It doesn't bear thinking about these days. I was forced to do strange, painful things which were considered normal; part of the day-to-day running of the school. When I think about the effect that has on a young person... today, young people have self-esteem, they're untouchable, they have a feeling they can't or won't be violated, or be belittled or be publicly humiliated. Myself, you, the other lads that went to that school, I don't think any of us will ever have a belief that we can't be violated. We know that we can be. Because we were. That was one thing that was ruined by that school. I don't think much about St Ambrose in terms of learning – I think about it in terms of a strange game-cum-battle that I had to deal with every day. It certainly wasn't there to develop me as a person... as a young man. With hindsight, it was quite awful what happened there.'

Derek Scanlan – who would later give evidence against Alan Morris in court – came to the school in 1979. 'I'd been at a fairly abusive primary school and I was looking for a way out, I suppose,' he told me. 'I asked my parents if I could go to St Ambrose. They thought I had no chance of getting in so they agreed to it – and I got in. I was appalled. It was worse than where I'd come from! You were beaten for academic failure. There was no protection, no guidance. Bullying seemed to be accepted. You were given far too much to do; you couldn't keep on top of academic studies. It was crazy. It was everything that could be wrong about education. You were treated like an idiot, even though you knew fine well you weren't. It was a selective school – there wasn't an idiot there. By the time you got to be about fourteen, you were beyond the violence. It almost became a competition to see who could get the most in a day. It didn't hurt anymore.'

'I was there between 1983 and 1988,' says former pupil Neil Summers, a TV producer who didn't give evidence at the trial. 'Corporal punishment – from getting a smack across the face to getting the leather strap – was the norm. The *lingua franca* was physical violence. I got grabbed by the throat by one teacher – it was just water off a duck's back after a few years. I can't remember how many times I got hit, it was so many.'

Former pupil David Prior, now a respected journalist, gave evidence against Alan Morris in his second trial. He was at the school from 1984 to 1995.

'Looking back, what stands out for me now is the old-fashioned nature of the place,' he told me. 'It seems a different world now. It was very much run by the Christian Brothers and yet the number of frankly odd teachers was incredible. You could say there were several teachers who would never get near a school now, ever. They wouldn't get through the front door. But because they'd been there for years and years and years, they were just part of the furniture. And I think the newer teachers just accepted these older characters and so they never kind of questioned the status quo and that allowed lots of very odd and sometimes abusive behaviour to happen.'

Ex-pupil and trial witness Andy Rothwell says, 'They tried to portray the school as a private school – they tried their very hardest. But it wasn't a private school. It was very disciplined and you were very fearful of the teachers. You couldn't really express yourself. You were only really supported if you were sporty or you were a high achiever academically. Beatings were on a daily basis. I didn't think anything of it. I thought it was normal. I didn't question it at all. I remember a brother chasing a boy around the class throwing punches at him. Punching him in the head!'

That private school ethos – that sense of being a 'cut above' that Tim Gresty describes from his experiences in the 1950s – was a part of what made St Ambrose unusual. There was also a demarcation inside the school based on money and class. Some pupils came from outlying areas and were largely there because they were bright. Some were from local families and were there because they were wealthy.

As DI Jed Pidd explains, 'At that time, St Ambrose was a fee-paying school and certain individuals were at the school because their mums and dads were fortunate enough to be able to pay the fees. But there were other pupils there as a result of bursaries. Those children and their parents thought themselves very lucky, in a very privileged position, to be at the school. By and large, it's these pupils that were the victims. They were the people Alan Morris picked on. They didn't want to rock the boat. They didn't want to say, "Hang on, I'm getting a good education here but something dreadful is happening to me."'

I recognised exactly the kind of aspirant, working-class boy that DI Pidd was describing. Because he was describing *me*.

CHAPTER TWO

A TRIUMPH HERALD
AND A ROLLS-ROYCE

I'd like to think I don't have a great deal in common with Alan Morris. But there is one thing that connects us: we both started at St Ambrose College on the same day.

At the start of the September term in 1972, I arrived for my first day. Morris had come to the school via a degree from Cambridge and his short-placement stint in Wythenshawe. I got there after being 'spotted' at my primary school as a child with potential. As the youngest of five kids from a terraced house on the wrong side of Altrincham, I wasn't natural St Ambrose material. Added to which, I wasn't even a Catholic – although my mum was.

'Your dad wasn't that bothered, it was more my idea,' my mother, Margaret Nolan, tells me more than forty years later. 'The headmistress at your infants' school said you were clever. And I wanted you to go to a boys' school to break away from what your four older sisters were doing. Your dad was out working all day and you were surrounded by women – you didn't know how to wee standing up! I remember going up to St Ambrose and asking how someone could get into the school. They said you had to sit an exam and, if you passed, you could go. They made it sound so glowing. The education you were going to get would take you to the moon and back. It was like an oyster opening up to your future. It's there on a plate: take it!'

I still remember when I went to the school to sit the entrance exam. So does my dad.

'It was one Saturday morning,' Ken Nolan tells me. 'When we arrived, there were all these Rolls-Royces and Jags – we had a Triumph Herald. As I parked next to them, I thought to myself, *What the hell are we doing here?*'

I sat in one of the prep school's wooden classrooms as they handed out the test papers. They were handwritten 'ditto machine' copies with that fruity, chemical whiff anyone of a certain age will instantly remember.

Some of the maths questions were beyond my grasp but the English was easy and, before long, it was break time. It was a breezy, sunny day and we were led out onto the fields next to the classroom. The greenery seemed to stretch as far as I could see – the school and its grounds seemed as big as the park at the bottom of my road. Bigger even.

One of the parents was helping out that day and had brought a huge bag of sweets. He threw them into the air, encouraging us to scramble around in the grass to catch them. Then it was back indoors for more easy questions. The way I figured it, if it was going to be like this every day, you could count me in.

I passed the exam and, after a swift Catholic conversion, arrived for my first day at St Ambrose dressed in the school's distinctive red and blue-striped blazer and cap. The first thing I became aware of was my accent. It was noticeably downmarket compared to everyone else's: a bit too 'Sowf Manchestoh'. A survival instinct kicked in and by lunchtime I'd changed it, making it bland and classless. I still speak that way today.

I fully bought into the school, the opportunities it was affording me and its Catholic church next door, the Holy Angels. The incense, the hymns and the echoing silence of it were beautiful and inspiring.

I became quite hard-line in terms of my newfound religion and remember being very disapproving of the 1973 Elton John hit 'Daniel' because it contained the line, 'Oh God, it looks like Daniel.' It took the Lord's name in vain – that was blasphemous.

Our form teacher in Prep One was a lay teacher called Mrs James, an astonishingly elderly and frail-looking lady who walked with a heavy cane with a thick rubber stud on the end. Early on in the first term, one lively kid was being too chatty for her liking. She grabbed him by the scruff of the neck, pulled him over a desk and beat him repeatedly across the back with her walking stick. He was seven. We were so shocked I don't remember any of us talking about it.

After all those years, I managed to track down another boy who was in my class. Paul Quinn is now a music-industry lawyer in Florida but he was sitting with me that day.

'What happened in the prep school was so grossly violent and so grossly unfair, so un-nurturing,' Quinn told me, as we spoke for the first time since we were sixteen. 'The culture of violence that existed was accepted and normal – almost a throwback to *Tom Brown's School Days*. It was terrifying. It was a daily thing. I used to be terrified of going to school every day. I can remember Mrs James beating that kid over a desk with her stick. He was the "bad" kid in the class; the "bad" seven-year-old.'

These shared memories, most of which I'd lost over time, began to tumble out of Quinn: 'Brother Healey – he would pick you up from your desk by the hairs on the back of your neck. You could hear them ripping and it would leave blood specks on the back of your collar. We had to sing, he'd walk around and, if he thought you were singing inappropriately, he would slap you and call you a crow. *Crow!* We were seven-year-old boys! Then there was the insanity of Brother Mullen.'

Mullen would play a game during his lessons involving the blackboard. At any given point, he'd gently tap a dot of chalk onto the board and shout, 'Where's the dot?'

It was to make sure he had the boys' undivided attention. He would then pick on one and invite him up to the front of the class to point to the dot. If you couldn't, you'd be strapped on the hand. You hadn't done anything wrong – it was entrapment. As he lifted the strap, Mullen would gain momentum by a few practice swings before delivering the blow.

'I remember getting strapped so hard by him I could no longer hold a pen, my hand would be so swollen,' remembers Quinn.

Once, at the end of a school day, Paul was getting on a bus when he saw one of his classmates knocked down by a car. He was distraught and went to tell Brother Mullen about what happened. In the process of telling the story, Quinn began to cry. Mullen strapped him for weeping.

'I was so terrified of him that I decided the best thing I could do was convince him I was a good guy and not worthy of his ire,' recalls Paul. 'So when he was on playground duty, instead of playing with my friends I used to spend my break time walking and talking with him. That's how I thought I could protect myself. Just thinking about it now catches in my throat. It was a childhood-ruining experience.'

Paul Quinn also reminded me about another boy in our class: Christopher Gore. Chris was a quiet, nervy kid who nearly always turned up to school in an unkempt state: greasy hair, dirty clothes and sleep dotted on his eyelashes. He had a temper and once walked out of school after he'd been pushed too far by one of the teachers. I was sent to chase after him to persuade him to return but I didn't manage it and he headed all the way home.

Chris went right through school with us, eventually pulling away from his peers academically as his genius for maths became apparent. He graduated at the very highest level but never achieved his full potential.

In 1991, Christopher Gore took an axe and killed both his parents. Investigating officers also questioned him about two other murders. In his trial, the court heard he'd been starved of love as a child and that his parents had overambitious expectations of him. He had an 'irrational and consuming hatred' of them, suffering severe mental issues since childhood, which carried on into his adult life. Chris was found guilty of his parents' manslaughter on the grounds of diminished responsibility and has been in Broadmoor high-security psychiatric hospital ever since.

Those beatings we took during our early schooldays were largely based on performance, rather than behaviour. There was no bad behaviour: when a teacher walked into a class, you stood up; when a teacher walked out, you stood up again.

There were also sections of the Catechism to learn – a pocket-sized red book containing hundreds of pieces of advice for entry-level Catholics. It covered everything from the Ten Commandments to 'What were the chief sufferings of Christ?' in a question-and-answer format. It also dealt with how you should go about your daily life, from first thing in the morning until last thing in the evening. It was the advice about what to do after you'd said your prayers at night that always stuck in my mind: 'After my night prayers I should observe due modesty in going to bed; occupy myself with the thoughts of death; and endeavour to compose myself to rest at the foot of the Cross and give my last thoughts to my crucified Saviour.'

Even at the age of seven it struck me as a deeply odd thing to ask a child to memorise. It was even odder to beat that child if he failed to remember it.

As well as beatings there was the weapon of humiliation; of being shamed in front of the other lads. I remember Brother Healey making myself and another boy stand in the middle of the playground as he screamed and shouted at us in his heavy

Irish accent. Our crime was bringing '*dorty, filty*' magazines into school. He waved them in the air, brandishing them to the heavens as he denounced us for bringing such sinful '*filt*' into school. The path of boys who indulged in such '*dorty*' magazines led, purely and simply, to hell.

The magazines were taken from us. They were *Spider-Man* comics.

'It's so absurd that these things were accepted as normal,' Paul Quinn says. 'It made us distrusting of people. And we can never get that back, David. I never slept as a kid. I still struggle now. I had terrible eczema – really bad – in the crooks of my arms, my neck, the backs of my knees. I don't remember it being bad before I went to St Ambrose. It was totally gone by the time I was nineteen and I've never had it since. I'm sure there's some sort of emotional and psychological connection. I want more to come out about the violence we all lived under on a daily basis. The validation of what happened to Alan Morris is tremendous for those who were his victims. For the rest of us, that whole sick and twisted environment that they called an education – and there's barely a teacher that can escape from this – I want to come out. If ever there was a place where God didn't exist, it was St Ambrose.'

This harsh, uncaring attitude towards such small boys seemed to be the accepted norm. Scott Morgan went to the prep school a few years after me and would later be a key witness in the Morris trial. He offers the following by way of example.

'I nearly lost my eye in the prep,' he told me. 'It was a pure accident. Someone swung on a tree branch, it came back and it went through my eye. My eye was bleeding, completely red. It happened at lunchtime and the teacher would not let me ring my parents or let me go home. Eventually, my mum picked me up and took me straight to hospital. They had to take my eyeball out to get all the splinters out of it... picking them out left, right and centre. I wanted to be a pilot when I was growing up – it destroyed that. My dad found out, went into the school and ripped the teacher's head off because she'd waited so long it had damaged the eye too much. That teacher was a monster in a different way, an evil cow.'

The prep school was essentially four interconnecting wooden rooms situated next to Woodeaves, where the Christian Brothers lived and occasional music lessons took place. The prep's shower and changing rooms were connected to the brothers' house. Each year you moved to the next room, with the same thirty lads as company. Those rooms were our world.

Despite the regular beatings, I began to shine at the school and, by year three, I was top of the class with an end-of-year report to prove it. After year four, if I passed the 11-plus I could go to the St Ambrose secondary school on an assisted place. No one gave it a second thought – I was clever; I would breeze through to the 'big school'.

'You passed the exam easily when you were eleven to go to the upper school,' my mum recalls. 'I was dead pleased. If you didn't pass, you had to go to another school, or you had to pay. A lot of them did pay. They had the money. The school had a good name.'

The prep was a fairly benign proposition compared to what

lay in store. We were worried enough about the big school to meet up on the first morning to walk together. We'd heard tales about bullying from the older lads – but we needn't have worried about the pupils, it was the teachers we should have been fearful of.

It became clear there was a dividing line between the local Hale Barns lads from wealthy families and poorer pupils who were on assisted places. The teachers seemed to treat us differently. There was one thing that marked me out as one of the 'poor' lads: the school badge on my new black blazer had bits of blue and red fabric where it had been cut from my prep blazer and sewn onto a cheap jacket to save money. I might as well have had a sign over my head.

The amount of corporal punishment dished out at the secondary school was ludicrous. There wasn't a single aspect of school life that wasn't tainted by it. Everything from getting a question wrong to turning around in class, or smiling, or anything perceived as defiance, was met with a beating. The strap, the slipper and the large wooden board compass were all popular weapons. Fury was the default setting for many teachers and pupils were often punched and kicked – properly punched in the face, that is.

'There was a lad who was hit by a teacher and got all his front teeth knocked out for talking in class,' remembers ex-pupil Scott Morgan. 'The teacher was an ex-boxer and smashed his head onto the desk. Nothing was ever done about it. It was just swept under the carpet.'

Physical punishment was the norm for everything and so it quickly became meaningless. In the second year, myself and another boy once held a competition to see how many times we could get hit in one lesson. The other lads cheered us on as the beatings mounted up; I managed to get slippered seventeen times but the other lad beat me with twenty-three. It was a double lesson, to be fair.

The violence dealt out by the staff fed, unsurprisingly, into the culture of the school. Bullying and fighting were rife. When a scrap broke out, the playing fields would empty as lads rushed to form a massive circle around the two protagonists, making it very difficult for teachers to break through. When a fight ended, the two lads would often emerge covered in spit – the other pupils would 'gob' at them as they fought.

The sheer size of St Ambrose and the surrounding fields made it impossible to police effectively and pupil punishment squads roamed the woods, handing out beatings and throwing smaller boys into an uncovered manhole in one of the lower fields. Once inside the hole, they'd be spat at or even have dead animals thrown at them.

Everyone seemed to smoke. Boys were so confident they wouldn't get caught that they'd often wander around the school smoking cigars, or even pipes.

When I reached the age of thirteen, Alan Morris took me for chemistry classes and then became my form teacher. His attitude towards me and many others can best be described as lascivious. When he wasn't raging at us, he presided over a *Carry On*-style atmosphere of innuendo and single entendre. When the talk became particularly fruity, his hand would go into his pocket and shuffle about as his speech went off at a tangent, far away from the lesson.

Tall, slim and shockingly strong, Morris would patrol the school with a distinctive walk created by the built-up brown shoe he wore due to his childhood polio. His brown leather bag contained his weapons, including a wooden spoon used to smack boys on the bottom. I was hit with this on many occasions. The vent of the blazer would be delicately lifted; the backside would be plumped to get it in just the right position before the smack was delivered. The vent was then delicately returned to its original position, again requiring more touching.

I recall once finding myself in the room behind the chemistry lab at lunchtime. Another boy was there – it was as if Morris had accidentally double-booked us. I remember thinking, *The classroom is empty; why are we being hit in this little room in the dark?*

Those unlucky enough to find themselves on their own with Morris remember the fear generated in the Dark Room. He would beat the boys, touch them and get them to take off their pants. Sometimes he'd tell boys to beat each other. Sometimes he'd even take pictures. But the key thing was the fear.

Ground Zero Boy, who was at the school at the same time as me, later testified how Morris described what he was about to do while whacking his cane on the walls and the furniture, ramping up apprehension in the Dark Room as much as possible.

'Alan Morris was the kind of character that you could have plucked out of Victorian England,' Ground Zero told me. 'That approach; that manner; that attitude to life; that attitude to people. He clearly lapped it up and enjoyed the whole charade of it. As we knew then – and as everyone will know now because he's in jail – he's a deeply twisted individual.'

'It's absolutely seared on my mind,' confirmed ex-pupil David Prior. 'He was just this stereotypical, almost horror-film character with his old blue [1970s] suit, a thick woollen thing with big shirt collars and the tie and the built-up shoe – everything about him was so creepy and fear-inducing for me.'

Mike Bishop was a pupil at St Ambrose from the late 1980s into the 1990s. He was one of Morris's victims and gave evidence at the teacher's trial in 2014. His memories are vivid, to say the least:

'He stank, he had dandruff all over his shoulders, he would always wear a waistcoat and had a huge instep on his shoe. All this, the way he dressed, acted, how he had this physical deformity from polio as a child, it kind of said, *There's something not right with him.* It's probably not the right thing to say about somebody these days but it made you think that it gave him the potential to flip. And no one wanted to push that button.'

Morris would often offer me a deal: a fierce punishment in front of other pupils or a lesser one away from the class at break time. But the idea that boys should steer clear of Morris at break time wasn't schoolyard chatter – it was vital information to be acted upon. Having found myself in the Dark Room once, I vowed never to go back again. I opted for the harsher version in front of the lads but my choice seemed to harden Morris's resolve to deliver an even firmer blow.

For me, the more the beatings continued at St Ambrose, the more I lost heart and slumped into despair. I remember once getting strapped by the headmaster and being told to sign a punishment book. *There's a punishment book?* I must have been hit a thousand times before and not once had it been logged.

In the third year of the prep I'd been top of the class. By now I was slipping towards the bottom. The one saving grace for me was drama and biology teacher Norman 'Sam' Wilkinson. Wilkinson 'scouted' me in the first year of secondary school during a drama improvisation class. As part of the improv, I stormed out of the class in a fury, which delighted him – he clapped his hands and stamped his feet with laughter.

So I was swiftly drawn into the inner circle of the St Ambrose stage staff, whose members got an array of special privileges. We were allowed to go to the front of the line at lunchtime, play music, smoke in the backstage club area and miss games if Wilkinson deemed there was an important task to carry out. I managed to skip games for a good eighteen months thanks to him.

I thought I was very special indeed. I wanted to become an actor and Mr Wilkinson promised to help me, inviting me round to his house to make short films with his Super 8 camera and to let me use his snooker table.

I started to appear in school plays like *Oh! What a Lovely War* and *The Wizard of Oz*. I played Dorothy – it was an all boys' school, remember – but I played her as a tomboy, wearing dungarees and sneakers. I was a boy playing a girl who acts like a boy – very clever, I thought.

We did several performances of *Oz* and, as reward for my hard work, Wilkinson gave me a bottle of red wine on the closing night, which was always the scene of a riotous backstage party. I polished the bottle off under his approving gaze; it was the first time I got myself massively drunk and I was ill throughout the following day. I was twelve, going on thirteen.

Although I took a vast amount of aggression from older lads – playing a girl clearly meant I was a 'puff' – I loved the attention the plays brought me. People knew who I was and my confidence – indeed, cockiness – began to grow. Punk rock was kicking off and I dyed my hair bright blond – the first kid in school to do so. It should have made be more of a target but it gave me a hint of celebrity.

My drinking at school also lent a certain cachet – I was carried unconscious from the Sunday-night youth club after downing a bottle of Cinzano – and being known as 'the kid who can drink' seemed to mitigate against being thought of as 'the puff from the plays'.

But I was desperately unhappy at home. With daily beatings at school and my parents dividing into warring factions, drinking was my escape. By the age of fourteen, my party trick was to turn up with a full bottle of vodka and have it emptied by the time the party ended.

At this time there was an incident at school that would change everything for me. Someone broke into St Ambrose at night and vandalised the stage area; the stereo was smashed, the curtains were torn and paint was thrown everywhere. The school was buzzing with speculation as to who was responsible and, despite the fact that I clearly loved school plays and cherished being part of the stage crew, the blame arrived at my door; not because someone had seen me, or my clothes had splashes of paint on them, but because I had dyed hair and liked getting drunk.

I was grilled for a week and the headmaster threatened to call the police. I *begged him* to call them – they'd see straight away I was innocent. At the end of that week, unable to prove I'd done it, he let me back into class but threw me out of the school theatre company. I never appeared in another production.

The final reason for being at school had been taken away and I gave up. For the last eighteen months, I sat at the back of the class, reading music magazines. The beatings continued but they didn't matter at all by this stage. I'd be sixteen soon. The end was in sight.

Despite (or perhaps because of) the harshness of school discipline at St Ambrose, there was a bizarrely humorous, anarchic attitude among the lads. The teachers were essentially saying, *Do this, or we'll beat you.* In return, the lads replied with, *You beat us this morning and you're probably going to do it again this afternoon... so we don't care.*

St Ambrose also had an unusually long lunch hour – nearly an hour and a quarter at its peak – and with acres of grounds to run wild in, when the lads cut loose, they really went mad. There was a feeling of invincibility in some quarters that led to a series of surreally complex stunts designed to flick the Vs at the school establishment.

Strange as it sounds, I've spent a lot of time laughing while interviewing ex-pupils for this book; laughing at the absurdly comedic way the lads fought back against the system. This was done in typical St Ambrose fashion – find the weakest and pick on them relentlessly – but, in this case, it was the weakest *teachers* being targeted by the pupils.

Less strict teachers would be subjected to the humming torture, whereby one lad started to hum a single monotonous note. A second pupil would join in, then a third. The noise would grow and grow but, because there were no outward signs, the teachers couldn't identify who was doing it. They would ask a suspect if he was making the noise; the lad would stop humming, say, 'Not me, sir,' then carry on. This could take up half a lesson on a good day.

Some classrooms had empty cupboards along one side. As the teacher was writing on the blackboard, boys would drop to the floor and crawl along commando-style to climb in. Slowly, class numbers would dwindle until the teacher went to investigate; sliding back the cupboard door, he'd find the inside compartments rammed full of lads.

Most of these acts of anarchy relied on co-operation, none more so than 'moving desks'. We'd wait until the teacher was busy at the board, then three or four pupils would swap places. The teacher would turn around but wasn't quite sure what was amiss, then turn back to the board as several more lads swapped. On the third occasion, the lads would just stamp their feet on the floor, making it *sound like* they'd moved. The teacher would quickly turn around, confident he'd rumbled what was going on, only to find none of the lads had shifted an inch. Genius!

At St Ambrose in the late 1970s, the big topic of playground conversation had been Skylab, the US space station due to come crashing to earth in the summer of 1979. So when the teacher's back was turned, we'd pick up our schoolbags, throw them in the air *en masse* and the cry would go up, 'Skylab!' Then all the bags would come crashing to the floor.

But the incident that sums up the lads' attitude best was described to me during the Alan Morris trial years later. An ex-pupil told me he'd passed the headmaster's office one day and seen a queue of his mates waiting to be strapped. Just for the hell of it, he joined the queue and took a beating for no good reason other than the thrill of fooling the teachers.

When it was discovered what he'd done, there was fury among the staff - but what could they do? Beat him again for taking a punishment he shouldn't have received in the first place? The incident showed the pointlessness of the punishment system.

Jogging alongside the anarchy was the sense that staff had no feeling of how it felt to be a teenage kid. One day, during games, one lad became ill and suffered a terrible bout of diarrhoea. It happened on the school fields and the lad in question was led to a tarmac space close to the changing rooms. Then the teachers turned a hose on him in front of the other pupils.

At the age of sixteen, I received a letter telling me my time at the school was done. There was no way I wanted to stay an extra minute anyway, so this was fine by me. As I was leaving, I was told to have a chat with the school's careers adviser, woodwork teacher Mr Hibbert. I went to see him in his workshop.

Mr Hibbert, a perfectly decent and kind man, asked me what I wanted to do with my life. Not really knowing what to say, I told him I wanted to be a journalist. Wearing his brown woodwork bib and looking over the top of his glasses, Mr Hibbert rifled through a card index on top of his workbench.

'You might as well apply for this then,' he said, handing me the details of a trainee journalist job available across town. I applied – and I got it. I've been a journalist ever since. Over the next thirty years I'd work in newspapers, magazines, radio and TV, and then I became an author. And it's all thanks to that card that Mr Hibbert gave me in the late spring of 1981.

(If it hadn't been for a member of St Ambrose's staff, I'd never have written this book. There's a tasty slice of irony right there...)

I had the job in the bag before I'd even taken my O-levels. As a result, I put even less effort into them than I was planning to. I never went to collect my certificates and, to this day, still don't know what qualifications I left school with. (I know it wasn't many.)

Starting my first job, aged sixteen, on *Link-Up* magazine was like waking up on a different planet. A matter of weeks before, if I'd made a mistake or been caught doing something I shouldn't have, I'd have been beaten. Now I was shown the right way and encouraged to try things for myself. I was listened to and treated pretty much as an equal. It was astonishing.

Why on earth had I put up with all that shit at school? What was I thinking? *One day,* I thought, *we should tell people what went on – but in the meantime, let's put it out of our minds.*

No one would be allowed to mistreat me again, ever. If I

had so much as a whiff of it, I'd strike first. Because I was so unused to being treated in a reasonable way, I was wary, touchy and verbally aggressive with many of the people I worked with, but amazingly, they were still nice to me. I was constantly on my guard, waiting for someone to rage at me, take a swing at me, but it never happened. The magazine staff taught me how to act, how to enjoy work and how to write. My proper life had begun.

At the end of my first week, my new colleagues took me for a 'welcome aboard' lunch at the Bull's Head, the pub across the road from St Ambrose. I was aching for one of my old teachers to walk in and see me in my new role – an adult, out of their reach, having a spot of lunch with my grown-up friends with a half-pint of bitter in my hand. I was untouchable.

Then, a week or so after I'd started work, my final school report arrived in the post. There were various half-hearted comments and wishes for good luck from teachers. Alan Morris had written just four words in his section: 'The Battle Is Over.'

Only it wasn't, was it, Mr Morris?

The job card from Mr Hibbert set me on the road to a career in journalism. And it was journalism that would take me back to St Ambrose nearly thirty-five years after I'd left.

Seeing a newspaper piece in 2012 about the arrest of a teacher over historical-abuse allegations stopped me in my tracks. No name was given but I rang the police straight away, knowing full well that the man they were dealing with was Alan Morris.

I remember coming off the phone and talking to my wife

about what I'd done. I even started to cry a bit – because I knew I'd have to go back to a time I'd long since put behind me.

They were tears of frustration, which would become a recurring theme over the next two years. I'd hated being a kid. *Hated it*. But now it was time to relive it all again. It was time to go back to the chemistry lab.

CHAPTER THREE

THE DARK ROOM

Alan Morris had an expression he regularly used; a favoured euphemism that many boys at St Ambrose knew the meaning of: 'extra lessons'.

'Come to the chemistry lab at lunchtime,' he'd say.

'Why, sir?'

'For extra lessons.'

The venue for these extra lessons was not the classroom but a dingy, windowless space behind the chemistry lab known as the prep room or, among the lads, the Dark Room. Inside the Dark Room, Morris would take a punishment that a normal teacher would dish out in a matter of seconds and stretch it out into a bizarre, ritualistic pantomime of fear. He would then use the punishment as a springboard for sexual assaults. The aim was twofold: to terrify the child and provide pleasure to the teacher. It rarely failed to achieve either of the desired effects.

Former pupil Andy Rothwell would later give evidence in Morris's trial. He was made to cane his schoolmates for his teacher's pleasure as Morris took photographs.

'He was the teacher that everyone feared,' Rothwell says today. 'I feared him more than anyone. Other teachers would run to him if things were going awry in the classroom. You'd then be asked to go in his room – the Dark Room – at lunchtime generally. You'd be beaten with a sort of table-tennis bat called the Paddywhack. We were also caned and given the strap. We were made to feel humiliated. He was a very imposing figure and looked down on you. It was a long, drawn-out process; he didn't want it to be a quick smack and that was it – it would be twenty minutes. He'd have you positioned over a stool and he'd make you very fearful over what to expect.'

Neil Summers was at the school from 1983 to 1988. He didn't come forward to police because, like many of the lads who went through St Ambrose, he'd shrugged it off as part and parcel of the experience.

'Morris was the Mr Big of the school in terms of punishment. Other teachers bandied him around as a threat,' Summers told me. 'He had a very menacing presence within the school – if Morris walked down a corridor, everyone was petrified. We were all scared of him. When he punished me, it was always away from anybody else in quite a secluded area of the school and he really took his time. One time he had me bent over a stool and I could just see out of the corner of my eye that he was methodically getting all his instruments out, quite ritualistically, waving things in the air, taking his time. He was messing with my head. Even as a child you'd think, *There's something not right about you.* As an adult now, with kids of my own, I can't believe grown men who were Christian were treating children like this. Even then it felt wrong but we didn't know any different. We were told to shut up and get on with it.'

There seemed to be specific types of pupils who would be targeted: they were often slight boys, petite, or outsiders and loners. Or sometimes they were the jokers; the kids that no one would believe. But many had one thing in common: they were usually the poorer lads who were, like me, at the school on a grant.

As DI Pidd says, 'I think that, to some extent, he saw the sexual and physical abuse he gave these children as some sort of payment for the education they were receiving at St Ambrose.'

Inside the Dark Room, boys would often be beaten as a prelude to molestation. One victim later gave evidence in the Morris trial that the teacher inflicted a fearful beating on him with a rubber Bunsen burner hose. The next time he found himself in the Dark Room, he braced himself, expecting the same treatment. But this time, a 'kindly' Alan Morris offered the child the chance to get off lightly: he was given the option of being hit with an open hand on the backside. He agreed, so Morris bent him over and smacked him but the hand remained touching the boy's backside and genitals as the schoolmaster pushed his erection against the pupil.

Other boys would later tell how he made them hit each other so he could watch – sometimes he'd take photographs or even film the event.

'He took four of us into the room and took a stool out,' Andy Rothwell told me. 'He held our hips. He gave the cane to me – it was a garden cane – I was the first. He then said, "Stand over there and hit your friend." He had a camera in his hand and held it up to his face. I started hitting my mate – I took a big swipe at him at first – *whack!* Morris panicked a bit. He said, "No! Not that hard. Gently like this, little taps..." He held my hand and showed me how to hit him. Then it was my turn and then it was another lad's turn, then another. We thought it was a laugh. He had his camera and he was stood about four feet behind us, looking directly at our arses. I'm shocked that it happened now. I look back and think, *Why did we allow that?* I imagine it was because it was an everyday occurrence. We didn't know anything different.'

The sexualised abuse of pupils wasn't always carried out behind closed doors – sometimes it occurred in front of a whole class. As Andy Rothwell says, 'When he was addressing you in front of other pupils, he generally went behind you. He'd put his hands on your shoulders and start massaging you. He'd stand on his tiptoes and start going up and down. Obviously he was rubbing himself up against our backsides. We didn't know. You don't realise at the time.'

It wasn't just the 'naughty boys' who were picked on by Morris; anyone got it if they took the teacher's fancy. David Prior, who'd later give evidence against Morris in his second trial, went on to be head boy at St Ambrose.

'He would sort of collar me after a class and say, "Come up to my prep room at break time,"' Prior told me, 'which I would – I didn't even question it. Then he'd shut the doors and it would be just me and him there. Then he would start doing his caning and his manhandling of me, turning me upside down, the Paddywhack stuff. He bent me over the stool, hitting my backside with the cane with a chalk mark on the end. I ended up being head boy – I wasn't a troublemaker, so it certainly wasn't a punishment thing, it was a pleasure thing for him. Sometimes he used the ruse of taking photos for the school magazine that were never seen, other times it was just a case of, "Follow me…" He did it on the quiet or when he was in isolation, so there was no one there to question it.'

In the 1980s, Morris ramped up his self-appointed role as the school's 'policeman', as he felt the headmaster at the time was letting discipline go to hell. Morris believed some of the pupils were 'evil' and that other teachers were relying on him to step in and keep order, as the school was in danger of 'going under'.

'At that time, we had a very weak headmaster called Brother Rynne… saintly man but very, very weak,' Morris would tell detectives during his police interviews. 'In that time, the discipline in the school went haywire. Absolutely haywire. In that period, I was form teacher to a fourth-year form and I stood outside the classroom while a young, very shy Irish graduate was trying to teach them maths. I stood outside, the noise was tremendous and I watched one object after another after another thrown at him, including a couple of wooden coat hangers, and they cheered when they hit him. I didn't actually intervene. When he came out, I still remember, he was wearing a pale blue-grey suit and his back was just covered in spit. That is the sort of Wild West the place became during Brother Rynne's headship.'

Rynne's reign as headmaster was brought to an end after a fire broke out at Woodeaves in 1983. Several of the brothers were badly hurt and one – a former teacher called Brother Doyle – died. Rynne was also injured in the fire and had to step down. Morris would later tell police he believed headmaster Rynne had accidentally started the fire himself with a discarded cigarette.

A new headmaster, Brother Coleman, took over in 1984. By now Morris and his methods stood out more and more. They had looked strange in the 1970s – midway through the more enlightened 1980s, they seemed positively bizarre.

Scott Morgan was at St Ambrose from 1979 to 1989. After the terrible accident with his eye in prep school, by now he'd moved up to the secondary school and, despite being academically gifted, he was struggling. His ear had been damaged at birth and the other kids called him Spock. He was also marked out as 'different' to other lads as his dad was famous: the former Manchester United player Willie Morgan.

'I had a breakdown at school because the abuse I used to get was systematic,' Scott told me. 'Three, four, five times a week. I was an easy target for Morris. He had his favourites and I think I became his single most favourite person in the school. I never cried. I never told anyone. I couldn't have mentioned anything at home because I don't know what my dad would have done. He's quite a fiery character.'

Morris would get Morgan alone and lay out a variety of his weapons of choice, taking great care and a considerable amount of time to choose the right one. At first, he'd simply hit the boy – but soon he was insisting that Scott take off his trousers and underwear and bend over a stool.

'When other teachers hit you, it was over in five seconds,' Morgan remembers. 'You knew it was going to hurt and then it was done and dusted. Morris was a creepy bastard. He'd walk you in slowly and methodically, he'd walk behind you, walk around you, make you sweat. It just got more and more perverse. Towards the end I was in there four times a week.'

It's a slightly crass question but I asked all of the lads if they believed their experiences at school had affected them in later life. For Scott Morgan, the answer to that question was a brutally frank one: 'After I left school, I tried to commit suicide twice – I've thought about killing myself probably another thirty times over the years. It made me an introvert. Everyone I come across finds it difficult to engage with me. I find it very difficult to make new friends. I wanted to get away.'

By now, Morris was beating and sexually assaulting boys on what police later described as an 'industrial scale'. The school's unusually long lunch break gave him ample time to carry out the attacks. Looking at the timeline of testimony from ex-pupils, he seems to have been carrying out his business of assaulting boys on virtually a daily basis.

The desire for privacy wasn't always paramount; by now he was getting other boys to watch him do it too. Another ex-pupil would later allege in court that Morris carried out a brazen sexual assault on him in front of several classmates. Sitting outside an Altrincham pub some thirty years later, this middle-aged man's voice still shook with emotion and fear as he spoke about it. As a boy, St Ambrose caused him so much stress that he literally pulled his own hair out in a state of nervous anxiety. He seemed as nervous now as he must have felt all those years ago.

'I remember clearly standing outside the chemistry lab, my heart pounding, looking through the safety glass,' Nervous Boy told me. 'I could see him talking to three or four other boys in there and I got called in and walked up to him through the lab. He said, "Why are you here?" I said, "You asked me to come here." He spent a few minutes going, "Oooh, let me think," and he started to go through a ritualistic sort of process: "What sort of punishment should we give?" Talking to the other boys and coming back to me. I was thinking all the time, *Why don't the other boys just go? Why are they still here? Whatever is he going to do to me?* I presumed I was just going to be hit at that stage; I didn't want it to happen in front of other people. I thought, *Just do it and let's forget about it, get on with it, just deal with it.*

'After a period of time, three or four minutes of asking them what punishment I should have, I went over. He was sat down on a chair. He said, "Kneel down," and he bent me over. I had to put my bum up and bend over his legs. I might have had to take my underpants off. I can't actually remember the physical sensation of flesh on flesh. Maybe I don't want to remember that, I don't know. But certainly I do remember lying there and being left there, again having to wait while he carried on his conversation: "What will we do with him now?"

'Then I remember his hands... feeling my bum and my buttocks. I assumed it was just him doing it but he could have got the other boys to do it as well for all I know. I was looking at the ground and focusing on a spot, just staring at the ground. He spent a long time – it would have been five or ten minutes – doing this but it felt like eternity. All the time he was talking to the other boys: "What else can we do to him?" They never said a word to him. Then he said, "Right, you can get up now and you can go." And I remember just getting up and I remember looking at the other lads. I felt fucking furious with them. I felt that, *Fucking hell, now I can't trust anybody. I don't even know who to trust anymore. No one's actually going to say, "Hey, this isn't right, what are you doing?"* So I lost confidence in the older lads and anyone who might stick up for the younger kids in the school. The other thing I do remember about it all was the relief that I had five or ten minutes left of lunchtime. I remember going out just thinking, *Thank God I've got time to play a bit of football.* It would have been worse to have gone back into a classroom after that, so there was some sense of, *Go out and run around for ten minutes to try and get over it.*'

Another ex-pupil, now a prominent businessman, approached police after Alan Morris was charged, claiming that he and another boy were told to beat each other while Morris watched, in the mid-1980s. Business Boy told his parents what happened and also complained about the incident to the headmaster.

'I'd probably been a bit naughty in class – nothing out of the ordinary – but I got beaten by Morris and he made me beat my friend,' Business Boy told me. 'He did it for his own sexual gratification – even at the age of fourteen we knew that was wrong. It wasn't right; there was an agenda to it, a sexual agenda. I complained to my parents and to the headmaster at the time, Brother Coleman. The whole thing was quashed. The school wrote to my parents saying they were going to kick me out. My parents didn't believe me. They put their trust in the school.'

The theme of Morris involving other pupils in corporal punishment sessions – and of complaints against him being smoothed over – crops up again and again. Derek Scanlan and Paul Wills, who both started at the school, aged eleven, in 1979 – gave evidence in his first trial. They remember being 'rounded up' by Morris for no apparent reason and taken to the chemistry lab. They were caned and then told to cane each other as the teacher watched.

'He was a looming figure,' Scanlan told me. 'I was always warned against him. Everyone was aware of him. The teachers were all abusive but the incident with Morris was sexual. That's what set him apart. He also had an arrogance about him – the others were just buffoons. He thought the whole thing was great fun. We hadn't even done anything wrong. He just rounded us up and got us to do all these crazy things. It was all a bit beyond us; we were small boys. We didn't understand. It's only retrospectively that I understood the sexual nature of it.'

As well as Morris's activities in the chemistry lab, Paul Wills also recalls the teacher touring the school changing rooms. 'He used to come around the showers at lunchtimes, walking around us, literally sniffing the air,' Wills told me. After one incident when he was touched and pushed against Morris's erection during a beating, Wills decided he would take no more. 'I was a fighter and I really went for him afterwards.

I spent the rest of my time at Ambrose going for him. I was raging, I really was. I remember going for the door after he'd been groping me and I thought, *I've got to keep this bastard away from me.*'

Wills took it upon himself to start abusing Morris with what he now admits were homophobic insults. 'It was really blatant. The other teachers heard it but there was no response. They'd look embarrassed or stony faced. The homophobic aspect was because I didn't have anything else to say; I didn't know how to put it: "Morris, you queer, Morris, you gay bastard!" that sort of stuff. I just wanted to keep him away from myself and my mates. That's the way it worked, you looked out for each other. Morris didn't react for a long time. You'd see him cringe if I came round a corner. He knew what was coming. He didn't react for ages.'

Morris did finally react after Wills warned another pupil to stay away from him – and his reaction was explosive. 'He attacked me. No warning. Quite professional, as if he'd done it before. He twisted my arm behind my back, pinched my neck and got me up to the chemistry lab. A lot of teachers were watching. One teacher was concerned and she was looking and watching, hovering around. He threatened me with the police but it was empty. He would have done it already if he was going to call the police.'

Derek Scanlan also remembers the teacher attacking Wills: 'Morris dragged him out and threatened him with expulsion and the police. He got very physical with him, gave him a beating. Paul warned the rest of us to stop saying things about Morris. It was just another day – another normal day.'

A fifth-form boy later claimed he'd confronted Alan Morris in 1985 and planned to go to the police about incidents he says took place in the Dark Room earlier in his school career. The pupil would later make allegations during the Morris trial that the teacher rubbed his crotch against the boy's head while he was bent over a stool, touching his backside on the pretext of checking whether he had anything down his pants to protect himself from a beating. He also alleged Morris told him to strip naked in the Dark Room as 'changing practice' after he'd got back late back from rugby. It's claimed by the ex-pupil that Morris tried to have him removed from the school but the boy dropped his claims after pressure was put on him from his parents.

Scott Morgan, who was by this time visiting Morris on nearly a daily basis, also remembers speaking out: 'One day I stood up to Morris – nobody did that – and he said I was going to get expelled. Morris went to Brother Coleman, the headmaster, and said, "Either Morgan goes or I go." Coleman turned round to him and said, "This boy hasn't done anything wrong; if you want to leave, leave." They were at loggerheads quite a lot of the time. We should have done something about it; we should have said something. I tried and I came very close to getting expelled. You put up with it because you knew it was a good school. "We are the best school and if you get thrown out, where are you going to go?" There was that fear factor.'

The school was clearly aware of the disquiet Morris caused. The teacher himself would later admit that the chairman of the governors, Colin Letting, was 'anxious' about the way the chemistry teacher was using corporal punishment. The governors spoke to Morris about this, circa 1986, but, again, nothing was done.

In another incident, Morris clashed with the school authorities after a row involving a pupil who refused to get his hair cut. Brother Coleman gave the pupil a deadline, which the lad ignored. This sent Morris into a fury, which he unloaded onto the pupil. Perhaps aware that he was running into trouble, the boy walked around the school with a Dictaphone and recorded Morris's diatribe. Morris was heard telling the boy he would 'chew you up and spit you out in little pieces.'

The boy played the recording to his dad, who complained, helpfully providing a typed transcript for the school. The deputy head had to visit the family and Morris was given a formal warning to be 'more careful'. Morris was scornful of their actions – he clearly didn't care what the school or the governors thought of him or his methods. He was more than a match for any of them, later describing the board of governors as 'weak' when he was being questioned by police after his arrest.

Despite these incidents, Morris continued his rise through the school hierarchy during the 1980s. He became head of chemistry, senior master and, astonishingly, head of discipline. The man who had already generated a string of complaints about his bizarre methods was put in charge of corporal punishment. He was effectively being fed boys by the other teachers.

As head of discipline, he would have been well aware of the Schools Act of 1986, which decreed that corporal punishment – in state schools and private schools receiving public money

– was to be outlawed. St Ambrose, as an independent school, didn't have to comply with the ruling until 1999 but decided to bring the ban in early, in 1987.

This would have been an extraordinary moment at the school – removing the very aspect that for so many years had defined it. But none of the ex-pupils I spoke to remembered it happening – there was certainly no announcement that anyone can recall.

As head of discipline, Alan Morris would have done what he always did when he disagreed with something – ignore it. Anyway, if there were new rules on the methods of discipline in the school, who would ensure such diktats were enforced? Why, the head of discipline of course.

'If you're head of discipline, it's like being head of the CIA,' says ex-pupil Mike Bishop. 'You can do whatever you want because you know you're not going to get touched, you're not going to be found out. I didn't even know that the ban on corporal punishment had happened. I didn't know to this day that it had happened in the mid-1980s!'

Some of the most strikingly odd assaults he would later be charged with occurred in the late 1980s, even into the 1990s. Morris clearly felt he was untouchable, perhaps unsurprisingly. Another direct complaint about his continued use of corporal punishment only led to him being 'advised' about it by the St Ambrose school governors in November 1989. Three months later, the minutes of the governors' meeting showed that Morris had promised he would stop using the cane; this was February 1990, almost three years after the school had banned corporal punishment in 1987.

Morris no longer even bothered to contain his activities within the sanctuary of the Dark Room. Anywhere in the school was fair game for an indecent assault.

The testimony of one of his victims, Mike Bishop, would later prove vital in prosecuting him. Bishop was a pupil at St Ambrose from 1986–94, the last of the intake to enter the school before corporal punishment was dropped. I spoke to Bishop after the trial – he decided he didn't want to be anonymous anymore and told me I could identify him. His memories of Morris remain strong to this day.

'I remember him being very tall – of course, we were smaller back then – but he was very commanding,' Mike told me. 'He had a lot of gravitas and a lot of presence. I remember being very, very scared of him. He sent letters to our parents when he became our form teacher, saying, "This is what we expect of your son. And if we don't get this, there will be repercussions." It was a case of: *You will not step out of line; you will do as you are told and, if you don't, so be it*. He never said what he would do; he just said there would be repercussions. And that was the scary part.'

Morris was Mike Bishop's form tutor in the second year and also took him for chemistry and religious education. Aged twelve, Bishop felt straight away that Morris was targeting him in a strangely overt, sexual way.

'He would sit on my desk, pull my tie out from underneath my jumper and start to curl it round his finger. Because he wasn't moving, I would move closer to him. He would do it slowly as he was talking, whether it was to me or the rest of the class. He curled it round his finger until I was literally half an inch away from his lower abdomen. Then he would let me go and push me back. It was never yanked, it was never pulled, it was never done in an aggressive manner; it was done very suggestively and it genuinely creeped the crap out of me.'

Bishop's classmates noticed the attention he was receiving and ribbed him mercilessly. He was, in their vernacular, Morris's 'bitch'.

'I got abused by the boys in the class because I was his favourite, got a lot of stick about that. I got into a couple of fights about it too.'

Morris would make Mike accompany him as he patrolled the school at break time, looking for boys inside classrooms when they shouldn't be. He would go through the rooms one by one, heading for a long outcrop corridor with a lone classroom right at the end. There was one such room on the first floor and one on the ground floor; cul-de-sac classrooms with one way in and one way out. Morris would check it was empty, that there was no one likely to come in and then close the door.

'That was the scary bit, that,' says Bishop with a shudder. 'I remember he'd turn around and look at you and start talking in that suggestive, very low tone – a soft manner. That was when he'd bend you over the desk and start to spank you and that was fucking horrendous.'

One of Morris's favourite tricks was to chalk a cross – a target – on Bishop's backside and smack him with his hand. He would then claim he'd missed the target and would have to do it again. And again. And again. Each time Morris's bare hand would linger on the target area.

Then there was the matter of removing the chalk mark. Morris insisted that he should rub it off himself.

'I was like, *Wow, what just happened? Why has this happened again? Why is this happening to me? What am I doing wrong?*' said Mike. 'I felt fortunate to be at the school and I resigned myself to the fact that this is just what happens. *This is just what school is like and I've just got to accept it.* But one day, when I had a good ribbing from the lads, I thought, No... *this can't be right; this shouldn't be happening.* One day I got home and fucking broke down. My mum said, "What's up?" I told her and she knew at that point that she had to step in and do something.'

Mrs Bishop rang Childline, the advice service recently set up to help young victims of abuse. Then she contacted the school and made a formal complaint about Alan Morris. They didn't tell Bishop's dad.

'My dad was a copper. If he'd known at the time, he would have killed him. That was the reason I didn't tell him. It was a huge strain on our relationship and it was difficult to manage. It's still not quite the same because he didn't think I trusted him enough to tell him.'

Overnight, Alan Morris's attitude to Mike Bishop changed. Instead of the touching and the tie-curling, he became a 'nasty bastard' – and Bishop was delighted.

'You know something?' says Bishop. 'I was thankful for that. It sounds crazy but he would yell and scream and shout at me. I'd much rather have that. I know it sounds horrible but I'd rather have been hit – hit with that rubber hose, hit with a cricket bat. I'd rather have that than what he actually did. By being nasty to me, it was as if he was saying, *How dare you tell, how dare you say anything, how dare you go behind my back and tell people? What gives you the right?'*

Despite the Bishops's complaint, the Christian Brothers seemed unable – or unwilling – to do anything about Alan Morris. But in 1991 St Ambrose got its first lay head-teacher, Eric Hester, who'd previously been involved with the state sector. The reign of the Christian Brothers as headmasters was over.

This would be the same year that complaints against Morris ended. Change was clearly in the air and many of the 'old school' teachers, including Sam Wilkinson, retired. One incident, in particular, shows just how much things were changing at the school and that the culture of silence was finally crumbling.

A pupil walked into a police station in Warrington in 1993, just after he'd left St Ambrose, claiming to have been targeted by a teacher - not Alan Morris - at the school. He also alleged he'd been the victim of sex assaults, both at the teacher's house and on school grounds. He was nervous, to say the least; the teacher involved had threatened that, if the boy went to the police, he'd kill himself.

Amazingly, it was another teacher from St Ambrose who had arranged the police interview and accompanied 'Police Boy' that day. 'The other teacher arranged everything,' the ex-pupil told me. 'He arranged the interview and met me in Warrington. My sole objective was to stop the other teacher having contact with children. It was unheard of to complain about teachers for sex abuse. I felt out on a limb. The teacher who came with me took a massive career risk [by] going against the school. He moved on from St Ambrose not long afterwards.'

Although he gave a statement to detectives, Police Boy decided he couldn't face going to court and the matter was dropped. The teacher he claims abused him quietly left the school.

'I had to do something but I didn't have the bottle to go through with a court case,' Police Boy told me in 2015. 'I still feel like I let the other teacher down. He contacted the police, he organised it, he took me to the police; he put his career on the line. I felt selfish. That teacher did the right thing twenty years ago. I was too immature to realise what a risk he took to help me.'

Meanwhile, there was still disquiet about Morris – unease about the furious letters he fired off to parents and his physicality with pupils. Corporal punishment may have been officially consigned to the history books but it was now the 1990s and Morris was still using it – and it was still sexualised.

The second of Alan Morris's trials would later hear claims that, in the early 1990s, the teacher was still getting boys to smack each other while he watched; getting them to make moaning noises as he smacked them himself; and taking photographs of boys from behind as they knelt on chemistry tables.

Perhaps sensing that his world was beginning to change, Morris began preparing for a change of career. Since 1989 he'd been travelling to Birmingham to study to become a deacon in the Catholic Church. In his youth he'd shown an interest in the ecclesiastical life and, in September 1992, he was finally ordained as a deacon – essentially as a number two to a parish priest – and took a vow of celibacy.

He carried on at St Ambrose though, appearing in school photos in his dog collar for his secondary role as deacon at the Holy Angels next door. But his role as school enforcer seemed to be drawing to an end – Morris asked the headmaster to relieve him of the burden of head of discipline. Or, in the words of the school governors and the minutes of their meeting in November that year, 'Mr Morris has relinquished the position of hatchet man since his ordination.'

Meanwhile, perhaps emboldened by the presence of a headmaster who wasn't a Christian Brother, it seems the St Ambrose school governors finally took some kind of action.

As one ex-pupil told me, 'My dad never liked him and he knew he was an odd man. Dad ended up being a governor at the school – he led the attempt to get Morris chucked out. The general dislike of the man himself convinced my dad that this guy needed to go. So he was the most vocal critic on the governors' committee at that time.'

What this parent and governor didn't know was that he had good reason to be distrustful of Alan Morris – because this teacher-turned-deacon had been taking his son into the Dark Room. The boy had never felt able to tell his parents.

'All the nasty stuff came out later,' the ex-pupil told me. 'Now, my mum and dad kick themselves. For whatever reason, they didn't know about what was happening with me and they hadn't done anything to stop it sooner. Why didn't I say anything at the time? Three reasons: the culture of the time – the fact that I was a twelve, thirteen-year-old boy, so how the hell was I supposed to know that wasn't what you're supposed to do between teacher and pupil? And also I was a shy kid: I did ten years of piano lessons; I didn't tell my mum and dad that I hated every single lesson, absolutely hated it. My mum used to say, "What did you do at school?" and I used to say, "Not much," or, "Can't remember." I wasn't one to come home and spill the beans about what happened at school. And knowing what kind of character Morris was too – there'd been an incident with him and my brother in the early 1990s, when another teacher had seen my brother doing an impersonation of Morris's walk and the teacher had reported this to Morris. He went completely crazy; he rang my dad at work and summoned both my mum and dad to his office. My mum says she remembers him taking his shoe off and slamming it down on the desk, making the point that this is what my brother was going to get. So it was a combination of those factors really.'

In 1995, Alan Morris says that he had a 'massive nervous breakdown' and contacted the school governors in November that year, asking for early retirement. They accepted. He then took up a full-time post at Holy Angels, the church so intrinsically linked with St Ambrose that it is, as far as many ex-pupils are concerned, on the school grounds.

For some of the lads who still lived locally, the decision to allow Morris to be deacon at the church just yards from the school gates was bizarre. It was made worse by the fact that, as some of them were churchgoers, they still had contact with him – albeit through gritted teeth. For some, it was too much.

'There was general astonishment that he went on to get the deaconship at Holy Angels,' ex-pupil David Prior told me. 'During my school years, my mum and dad still went there; we were weekly Catholics. So he started appearing on the altar a bit more, which was always a deeply uncomfortable experience. What then made it worse [was that] my nana – my dad's mum – lost her husband and moved into a little granny-flat part of the house. She was a weekly Catholic as well but Morris managed to gain her trust. So on a fairly regular basis, he would come to the flat to give her communion, when she couldn't get to church. She was in her nineties. He had a white car and, as he would come down the drive, general shivers would go down my spine. I would do anything to avoid him. When my nana died, we found out that he would be taking the service and my brother and I said to my dad, "You've got to stop that man being anywhere near the altar." I went to Holy Angels, saw the priest and said, "I've got to request that Morris doesn't serve at my nana's funeral."'

Nervous Boy also had reason to revisit Holy Angels. He admitted to me he'd had a panic attack at the thought of having to see Morris again at the church where he was deacon.

'My sister told me she was getting married... at Holy Angels church. I remember feeling the sickness and nausea and thought, *Oh God, how am I going to tell her I can't go back in that church again? I might have to stand outside.* Then I thought, *Fuck it. I'm not going to let him ruin my day with my sister, I'm just going to stand and look at him. I'll make myself look at him all the time.* So that's what I did. I just stared at him so he couldn't have any power over me or make me feel scared of him.'

To some ex-pupils, many of them by now family men, it seemed like Deacon Morris was taunting them from the pulpit, piously posing as a pillar of the church and of the community while both they and he knew the real truth. His control over the lads continued, despite the fact that his days as a schoolteacher were long gone. He'd found the perfect way to torment them further – from the pulpit of Holy Angels Roman Catholic Church. He even baptised some of their children.

'I would say that, in my experience – very nearly thirty years of policing – he's almost unique,' says DI Pidd of Greater Manchester Police. 'First of all, there's the lack of empathy towards his victims. Then there's his arrogance. I don't see a man filled with remorse and I don't see a man that actually recognises that what he did was wrong, unethical and unlawful.'

Life would stay on an even keel for Deacon Alan Morris during the late 1990s – it revolved around Holy Angels, his connections with interfaith groups, charity work and life at his home in Rivington Road, Hale. After the death of his mother, there was just him and his brother, Kevin; Morris would effectively become his brother's carer. But the calm facade couldn't last forever.

The first brick in the millpond was thrown by Ground Zero – who, after he became a parent himself, finally decided to do something about what happened to him as a schoolboy.

'I never forgot Alan Morris,' he told me. 'I still think of my schooldays every day. So he was always there – what came together in my mind was the reality of my own life. The catalyst was having a child myself and working in the health sector. When you put those two together, it's blindingly obvious. Something had to be done.'

Oddly, Morris and Ground Zero had experienced intermittent contact over the years. Ground Zero had contacted Morris to seek help in finding old films of him that had been shot by Wilkinson. Morris contacted another former colleague about this but nothing was found.

By 2001 Ground Zero had put such polite exchanges to one side – he wanted action. His first idea (though certainly not his best) was to turn up unannounced at Woodeaves, looking for his ex-teacher.

'Initially, I never thought of ringing the police,' he explained to me. 'As far as I was concerned, it had fuck all to do with anybody. It was my beef with Alan Morris.'

So one night Ground Zero knocked on the door of Woodeaves, asking for his former teacher. 'I was composed and rational. My head was switched on. The door opened and a little old housekeeper opened the door. I introduced myself and said I was looking for Alan Morris.'

The housekeeper told Ground Zero that Deacon Morris was normally to be found at Holy Angels Church these days. 'At that moment, a Christian Brother – an ex-boxer – appeared. He'd once punched me in the face in front of the whole class. He'd gobbed me. This brother was a foot shorter than me now – he must have been eighty-something. Despite this, I absolutely shat myself. I went to pieces. I couldn't help it. I scurried away.'

His next idea was to cover Hale Barnes village in posters, with a picture of Morris and a description of what he'd done. It didn't come to anything, so Ground Zero decided, instead, to ring Holy Angels and speak to Morris man to man.

'I wanted to tackle him, so I phoned the guy direct and the answer I got was, "I'm sorry, he's taken a group of schoolchildren out for the day." *Ping!* The penny drops. This man cannot be with a group of schoolchildren in a park because he's a fucking pervert! So I called the cops. I realised that I had to stop Alan Morris for the sake of everybody. Not for my sake.'

Ground Zero, by now living on the south coast, contacted his local police station. An officer was sent round to see him and he gave a thirty-two-page statement about events at St Ambrose. To back up his story, he gave the names of two other pupils who'd seen much of what went on. But the police came back to him and said the two ex-pupils had refused to help. So it was now his word against Alan Morris's – and the matter would be taken no further.

This was when Ground Zero and Morris would play out their telephonic chess game, with the ex-pupil trying to solicit acknowledgment of guilt from the deacon as he headed towards Hale Barns in his car. When he got what he wanted, Ground Zero stopped and went home.

In the meantime, however, clearly rattled by what had happened, Morris contacted his bishop, Brian Noble, and his solicitors, Rhys Vaughan, based in Longsight, Manchester.

For years all would remain relatively quiet. Deacon Morris returned to his dual life at Rivington Road and Holy

Angels; those who knew about his brief brush with the law kept silent.

But there was one other moment that surely must have rattled him – in 2007 former drama teacher Sam Wilkinson died. Morris had been at his former colleague's deathbed and would preside over the funeral. Ground Zero had been extremely fond of Wilkinson and decided to attend. After the service, he approached Morris and introduced himself. Despite their telephone exchange in 2001, the pair had not seen each other for more than twenty-five years. They then had what both have described as an amicable conversation.

Despite this strange encounter, everything remained calm for the ex-teacher – until one night when a doctor had one drink too many, in a bar about a mile from Deacon Morris's home.

Then all hell broke loose.

CHAPTER FOUR

A FAUX PAS

Despite all the long hours, hard work and dedicated detective skills that would be factors in the arrest and prosecution of Alan Morris, the core reason he is behind bars today is an awkward social situation in a bar in Hale, the neighbouring village to Hale Barns.

In late October 2012 a man was taking a drink in the American Bar & Grill on Ashley Road in Hale Village. He's an ex-Ambrose pupil and is now a general practitioner, so we'll call him Doctor Boy. He spotted another ex-pupil in the bar and, being a polite sort of guy, said hello.

'I went out for a drink in the American Bar and saw an old schoolmate who was in my year,' Doctor Boy told me in 2014, at a bar just a few yards from where this all happened. 'We weren't friends at school. I didn't like him, he didn't like me; he was a bit of a scrapper. I was a Man United fan; he was a

Man City fan. He was a difficult kind of guy. He was a Manc, I was a southern import. But, by now, we were older. By way of an olive branch, I was talking to him about school and I said, "Do you remember Morris? What an awful teacher he was – a violent, nasty man."

'I said to him, "You were always in trouble; you must have been in the backroom of the chemistry lab every day..." and I saw his face drop. I realised I'd made a *faux pas*. I said, "You must have had a horrible time at his hands." He didn't say anything but he looked *awful*. I knew by the look on his face. So, trying to be nice, I said, "Do you know what" – this is after a couple of pints – "you'll never guess what happened to me..." And I told him my story.'

The story Doctor Boy told his fellow ex-pupil that night changed his life and it resulted in Alan Morris being behind bars today.

'In sixth form, I'd changed from doing languages to doing sciences because I wanted to become a doctor,' he says today. 'I was doing badly at chemistry and I was offered "extra lessons". I was invited round to Morris's house for additional tuition. We lived in the same village so I ended up going round to his house in Rivington Road. It wasn't quite the chemistry lesson I'd expected. It was a bizarre and frightening experience.'

Arriving at the house, Doctor Boy was ushered into the living room. There was a television and a VCR with two armchairs. He was invited to take a seat. Alan Morris was then strangely silent.

'I was invited to sit in the right-hand armchair and he sat in the left. I can't remember any conversation; he just went over to the video recorder and put a video on and sat back down. I don't know what I was expecting – maybe a chemistry tutorial video or something. What came on was two young men in the woods – like a cub-scout video – engaging in homosexual activity. They were undressing and fondling each other. I took a glance to my left and Morris had started masturbating. I remember thinking, *What the hell is going on?* I was feeling utterly terrified. Then he basically tried to encourage me to join in. I remember being so frightened that I thought I'd better play along with it. I was so out of my depth. I thought, *I'm going to get raped – something hideous is going to happen.*'

Doctor Boy did a calculation: he figured that, if he allowed Morris to 'finish', it was unlikely that the teacher would be in any position to do anything else. Then the teenager could make his escape.

'He had a tissue in his left hand and he sort of finished up,' he says today. 'He switched the video off and I thought, *I really have to get the hell out of here.* I was so stunned by the whole thing I can't even remember how I got out of the house. I was utterly terrified by the whole experience; I felt so hideously powerless. It was all done in silence – a very mysterious process – and, before I knew it, I was in this situation I had no control of. It was like being in a fight at school. You're in survival mode: *how do I get out of this, how do I sort it?* I played along with him to make it go away. I was quite analytical about it. I thought, *He's a big guy, what can I do? If he ejaculated, he can't rape me.* I remember thinking that clinically, that carefully, about it. I'm rarely in a powerless situation now but the escalation from nothing to complete submissiveness, complete powerlessness, was utterly terrifying, quite frankly. To this day, I dread powerless situations.'

Doctor Boy can't remember how he managed to get out of Alan Morris's house that day. But he does remember that he went to tell his mum and dad.

'I went back home and spoke to my parents. I was elated that I'd got out of the house in one piece. To be fair, I was a bit of a joker at the time; I think maybe they thought I'd embellished the truth, [or that it was] a total bullshit thing; that I'd lied. "That's ridiculous," they said. "How could that possibly have happened?" My dad made the decision not to report it; he told me I'd had a lucky escape and that I should put it behind me. I did and got on with my life.'

Could it really be true that Doctor Boy's father wasn't convinced by his son's story? I spoke to the man it seems logical to call 'Doctor Dad'.

'I believed him about 90 per cent,' Doctor Dad told me. 'He has an ability to exaggerate; he's a bit gung-ho. We used to do a lot of things together; then, when he was telling his mates, it was always somewhat bigger than I remembered. [But] I believed him. Now you might say, why didn't I do anything? I didn't think that particular incident warranted it. [Doctor Boy] was embarrassed. His mother's worry was [that] people might think we were extremely irresponsible not to have done anything about it. No. If there's a significant problem here, other people will have had other experiences. Morris didn't lay a finger on him. As soon as he saw what was going on, the key objective was to get out of the place. What was on the video? Eighty-five per cent of the male population of the

UK will have watched some sort of porn – [this was] mild, homosexual porn. I thought we were on a hiding to nothing. If Morris has been molesting pupils, we had no evidence of it. We ran the risk of trying to run a flag up a pole that didn't exist. I was more than 90 per cent sure that an event took place that was embarrassing to my son – the other 10 per cent was… well, what was the content of it? How serious was it? I've been accused of being disloyal to my son. I wouldn't want to be loyal to someone who'd told a lie. Loyalty is a much overrated virtue. It's not a useful moral virtue. It's a prejudice that someone I know is good and the other one is the baddie.'

Back in the American Bar & Grill in 2012, Doctor Boy finished his story about what happened at Rivington Road all those years earlier. If he'd been expecting a reaction from his fellow ex-Ambrosian, he was to be disappointed. The other man left and Doctor Boy thought no more about it, until he got a phone call from another former pupil a few days later.

After the American Bar conversation, the man he'd spoken to had contacted a third party – an ex-pupil who was involved with the Holy Angels Church, where Alan Morris was now deacon. He'd been horrified by what he'd heard and had decided to share it.

'This guy said, "I've contacted the diocese social worker about what happened to you." He'd dobbed me in. This other guy's kids worked the altar at Holy Angels where Morris was the deacon. Then the social worker rang me and said, "Can we meet?" Now, I'm a GP, I understand the concept of sharing information. I know I'm done and dusted. At that point I have to make a decision: did I misremember it? Was it for real? What do I do? I knew a world of hurt was on its way.'

The diocese that had received the call was Shrewsbury, which actually covers large sections of Merseyside, Cheshire and part of Greater Manchester, as well as the county that it's named after. The diocese social worker at the time was Pauline Butterfield. She arranged to meet Doctor Boy at the Bowdon Hotel, close to Hale Village, listened to his story and then told him about the accusations made against Morris by Ground Zero Boy in 2001. Doctor Boy was shocked.

'She said, "We've had our suspicions about Morris for a number of years but we've never been able to put our finger on it. Do you have any information?" And I thought, *I've got a public responsibility*. I think about his position of power and responsibility within the Catholic Church. *I've always had a responsibility here and I've let it lie for twenty years.* I start to feel Catholic guilt, I start to feel disgrace. I thought, *Let's do what should be done and what is right.* So I tell her. She says, "You know I have to share this with the police?" Of course I know that.'

'In one sense, he was the guy who blew the whistle,' confirms Doctor Dad. 'He'd been in a pub where he got a bit pissed and someone else had grabbed that information and put it into a different context. They went to the church authorities and the question was asked of him: "Are you prepared to substantiate this?" Then he's asking himself, *Am I putting Morris in a situation he shouldn't be in?* He doesn't know if he's guilty of anything other than wanking off in his presence. How bad is that? He's also not sure it was something he wanted to go through, so he wrestled with that. Then he decided he had a responsibility to do something.'

'Anybody that comes forward has a lot of courage and I respect that,' praises DI Jed Pidd. 'Historical cases of abuse are really important because people need to go through a process of recovery and that process often starts with someone believing them, telling police what went on.'

'I was a reluctant witness,' says Doctor Boy. 'I didn't really want to be involved in this. I worried about my children. When I got dragged into this, I thought about what the consequences might be. I knew it meant two years of utter pain, distress, drink, sleepless nights and misery. My life's full of that anyway! I did think, *You owe this to yourself and you owe this to other people because you didn't do what you were supposed to have done all those years ago. You haven't helped anybody.* I feel bad about what I haven't done over the last thirty years.'

Doctor Boy agreed to co-operate and speak to the police. What happened next would kick-start the biggest historical-abuse investigation Greater Manchester Police had ever mounted.

CHAPTER FIVE

THE DIRTY DEAN
OF DISCIPLINE

If you were asked to pick the police detective out of a line-up of people from different professions, you probably wouldn't point to DC Barry Conway. He has the round-faced look and gentle tone of a kindly butcher, rather than a cop.

On 2 November 2012 Barry's line manager had been divvying up her caseload as she was being transferred to another division. She'd approached him at his desk at the Child Protection Unit, a nondescript house just behind Altrincham Police Station on Barrington Road.

DC Barry Conway: 'She came over to me and said, "How much work have you got on at the moment? Do you mind looking at this for me? I picked this job up last week. Have a look at it; it looks quite interesting." And it was Alan Morris. It was right at the early stages, following the information that came through from the diocese after the initial contact from the ex-pupil. The priest at Holy Angels had got involved with the child-protection officer for the Diocese of Shrewsbury, who then contacted the police. So it was a referral from the diocese. I said, "Yes, I'll take that on board" – little knowing what would happen next.'

The first problem Barry had was the rather convoluted route the information had come. It had passed through five different sets of ears before reaching theirs and there were no guarantees that Doctor Boy would talk, let alone give evidence.

'We didn't know whether he wanted to speak to the police or not,' says Conway. 'So it was quite delicate as to how we approached it from a professional point of view as well as a personal point of view.'

Because Morris was still in a position where he had regular contact with children, as deacon at the Holy Angels Church, time was of the essence. They didn't want to scare Doctor Boy off by coming on too strong but they knew that they had to act quickly because of Deacon Morris's position.

'Safeguarding children is paramount to everything we do,' Conway told me. 'It overrides everything, even an investigation, even taking people to court. Because Morris was within the church, it was important for us to address his position because he's got access to children: christenings, Sunday school, communion, etc. That was the reason the original person went to the diocese, because his children were at that church and going to communion lessons. So that takes precedence over everything else.'

Meanwhile, Doctor Boy was still wrestling with his conscience over what to do after that night in the American Bar. 'Morris retired quite soon after I left school,' he told me. 'So a bit of me thought, *Well, he's not in a position of power anymore.* That made me feel bit better. But when I remembered he was the deacon at the local Catholic church, it did make me think, *Is he still taking altar-boy lessons? Are there other issues here that haven't been properly addressed?* I was worried that, in the last fifteen or twenty years, someone might have been assaulted. That's what worried me the most. I said to myself, *This happened to you. Why didn't you do anything about it? Why has the forty-one-year-old with so much more information not reflected on what happened to the seventeen-year-old and done something about it?* Why, why, why, why, why? I struggled with that for ages. Then I thought, *I'll do it, it needs to be done. If nothing happens, I'm clearly barking up the wrong tree. But let's do it* – and if no one stands behind me, I'd look like a bit of a dickhead but that's life. But if there's one other person out there who has something to say, that's got to be beneficial, hasn't it? So I went for it.'

Doctor Boy gave a statement to police about what happened that day at Rivington Road. He also told of other incidents that occurred at St Ambrose – including further bizarre encounters with Alan Morris. On one occasion, when he was twelve or thirteen, Doctor Boy got into trouble after a fight with another pupil. He and the other boy were taken up to the room behind Morris's chemistry lab to be punished. They were expecting a severe beating – but that wasn't what he had in mind. They couldn't believe what they were told to do while their chemistry teacher watched.

'We were made to smack each other,' Doctor Boy told me. 'I smacked him, he smacked me. Neither of us was up for it – we'd just been in a fight. There was tension in the room; intense fear. There was a feeling that it was unusual, that it didn't fit. I knew afterwards that I could never go back in that room again.'

Doctor Boy also told detectives about other strange things that happened at St Ambrose: 'From the sixth form, we could see directly into the chemistry lab and see Morris with these first and second years, doing experiments. We'd see a child kneeling on a stool, with Morris taking photos of the boy with his bum in the air. We all laughed and said, "For God's sake, look at that, what's he doing? This is ridiculous!" I remember one time he saw us looking and let the blinds down because he was horrified that we had seen him. He knew that we knew. But the degree of control was so extreme that I don't think anyone was prepared to do anything about it.'

What impressed the police straight away was how believable Doctor Boy's story was. Here was a professional man – a general practitioner – telling them in clear terms what had happened to him and also recounting other odd incidents at St Ambrose.

'We have to be open and objective as investigators; we have to be down the middle,' DC Conway says. 'However, when you have such a credible witness coming forward and telling you something in such detail, in an eloquent manner, it does improve the evidence – it stands to reason. So he was a credible witness giving a very accurate account of what happened to him as a young man. But at that point, all we had was that one person.'

Barry Conway's boss, DI Jed Pidd, felt they were on the verge of something major: 'It struck me immediately, from what we were hearing about Morris, that he must have had access to hundreds, possibly thousands of children over the years. So if we'd got one complainant, it was highly likely we could have any number of complainants. Over the months and years since then, that's exactly what we've found. As is the case with a lot of former pupils at St Ambrose, this witness was a highly educated, highly credible individual. And it just smacked of, "This must be the truth." That's not to say we don't believe all our victims, because we very clearly do, but this individual was so credible [that] I thought this must be the tip of the iceberg.'

Like many boys who had gone to St Ambrose, Doctor Boy knew there would be many more pupils with stories to tell. The question was, would they come forward?

'My "spider sense" told me there would be other people, surely,' he told me. 'But will they stand behind me? Or will they do the Catholic schoolboy thing, which is to shut up and pull away from it in fear, as I have done for twenty years or more.'

Meanwhile, officers worked out their tactics for tackling Morris. 'Initially, there was a lot of discussion about how we were going to deal with it,' says DC Conway, 'because there are lots of different routes to how we deal with historical-abuse allegations. Sometimes we don't always arrest, we might bring them in for interview – under caution, not under arrest. So there are a lot of considerations to be made. But then the decision was made that we were going to arrest because we wanted to search his address and we can search at the point of arrest. We don't need a warrant – under the Police and Criminal Evidence Act, we can search his address and that's what we did because we were looking for other supporting evidence.'

At 1.35pm on Friday, 9 November 2012 police paid a visit to Deacon Alan Morris at home in Hale. 'We knock on the door, Mr Morris answers, we introduce ourselves, we go in,' is how Conway recounts the events of that day. 'He didn't really say a lot and he sat down in his living room. His brother Kevin was there but he was in a different room. We took Morris to his back living room and explained who we were and what we were going to do and then arrested him for the offences, giving him the usual cautions and explanations. We arrested him on suspicion of possessing indecent images of children and the indecent assault of a male, born out of the initial account of that first witness. So, at that point, we started to do the search – but he had so many books in his study [that] we had to get more people down to conduct the search for us while we took Morris to the custody office, which was at Pendleton. Because of the way everything has been restructured at Greater Manchester Police, our custody area for detention is in Pendleton in Salford.'

As Morris was transported over to Salford, officers continued with their search of Rivington Road. 'There were a lot of memory sticks and CD-Rs, a laptop and computer towers, DVD-Rs, VHS tapes and a camera – there were in excess of fifteen exhibits taken in total,' DC Conway recalls. 'Pen drives, laptop, mobile phone, discs – it's just a case of seizing what you think may become relevant, look through that and take it from there.'

Despite calling at Rivington Road at lunchtime, detectives didn't start interviewing Morris until 9.30pm that evening, as they had to wait for his solicitor to turn up. The initial interview lasted less than two hours. There wasn't a great deal to put to him at that stage, as all they had was the statement from Doctor Boy.

The ex-pupil's account was put to Morris, along with his accusations about taking photographs of boys and the sexualised nature of the beatings administered at St Ambrose.

'We talked in quite a bit of detail about what the witness said and then we asked general questions about sexual interest in children when conducting discipline. What was covered was only general because we had no specifics and no real evidence in relation to that. He was extremely defensive, [it was] a total denial of any wrongdoing, [and he] wouldn't accept any of the evidence that was put before him. He was very cocksure of himself.'

Officers went through the list of items seized at Rivington Road with Morris although, at this stage, none of it had been looked at. He was asked to confirm which items belonged to him, if there was any illegal material contained within them and whether any of it was pornographic. Morris told detectives they were 'theological' items that related to his work at Holy Angels. He did, however, admit a fondness for what he described as 'hunky' magazines.

The interview finished at 11.20pm. Conway drove Morris back across Greater Manchester to Rivington Road. There was silence in the car throughout the journey. Morris was given a bail sheet and told by officers that they'd be in touch.

The next day, the first task was to go through material seized at the house – the items Morris claimed were church related. The high tower and laptop were sent away to a specialist computer unit. The remainder was left for officers at Altrincham to sift through.

DC Conway picked a disc at random, put it into a player and started to watch. A title sequence came up on the screen – the film was called *The Dirty Dean of Discipline*.

'Out of all the exhibits, that was the first one and that just set the scene for all the others,' Conway later told me. 'The theme being teacher-pupil discipline scenarios that led onto homosexual acts, anal sex, down to extreme porn above and beyond that. From mutual masturbation, oral sex, to anal sex, fisting of anuses – that was what was involved.'

DC Conway spent the whole day watching every item that was seized. After all, Morris had assured officers there was no pornography to be found, yet the titles they discovered included *Prisoner of Pain, Sore Time Sebastian* and *Big Brother Spanking*.

'There were all kinds of sexual acts in these films but the main starting point was always discipline: the spanking of bottoms and the discipline scenario of pupil and teacher. However, they were legal pornographic films. It was quite obvious that they were adults and the films had been professionally made with the normal warnings, consent and the FBI information that you get about the age of the performers. But it was the volume of it. Particularly considering we interviewed him the night before and he was adamant that he didn't have any pornography, that we wouldn't find anything apart from these magazines that he said he looked at. I had to sit through all that, to make sure there was no child pornography – virtually a full day reviewing those exhibits, as that's what we were looking for primarily. In the end, we didn't get that but what we did get supported the case, in my eyes, without any shadow of a doubt. It showed interest in that subject matter of what we're dealing with. Because it's quite a specific MO [*modus operandi* – method of operation], very niche, I suppose. It was just the level of it.'

Viewing such material is a regular occurrence for officers like Barry Conway. The items Morris had were all legal but they also have to watch videos at the darkest end of the spectrum. I asked Conway how he copes, given that such material is believed to 'deprave and corrupt' those who view it.

'Investigations into child pornography are what we do a lot anyway,' he said. 'It's something you get used to. It's not nice but it's one of these things that just have to be done. So you've got to deal with it as coldly as you possibly can because, if you sat and thought about it, it would have an effect. It's about being as professional as you can and doing it as best you can really. Unfortunately, we have to look through a lot of these images because we have to view them as part of the investigation and, ultimately, put it before the court. But in the Morris case, it was different because it helped in a different way. What we were looking for originally we didn't get but what we did get back was just as impactive.'

Not only did it mean Morris hadn't told officers the truth, it also provided an indicator as to his tastes and tallied with the kind of teacher-pupil scenarios Doctor Boy had mentioned in his statement. Examinations of Morris's computer also revealed Internet searches for sadomasochistic forums and websites, as well as for words like 'school', 'spank', 'discipline4boys', 'cane' and 'schoolboy'.

Meanwhile, the police pulled out the file on the allegations Ground Zero Boy had made in 2001. He'd told officers of being beaten and touched by Morris in the Dark Room on a regular basis and about how Morris teased out the punishments to make the boy as fearful as possible, as well as inventing excuses to put items down his underpants. The strands of the investigation were starting to tie together.

By now, another officer had come into the investigation. Blonde and upfront, with glasses permanently glued to the top of her head and a voice like a foghorn, DC Nicola Graham became the 'people person' of the team. Graham, who can get along with pretty much anyone, was born and bred in the Altrincham area. She knew the place and the people who live there inside out.

Nicola describes Barry Conway as her 'work wife'. 'We are massively different people from different backgrounds in every possible way,' admits Barry. 'But I think, as a team, especially for this case, it worked perfectly. I've got the organisational skills to get everything ready and to make sure that everything is right. She brings the more personal side – I'm making sure everything is right so it all goes like clockwork, where Nicola is good at the emotional contact stuff.'

'Barry is the admin man,' says DC Graham. 'He pays attention to the details, filing everything in just the right way. He's very meticulous. Barry knows he's verging on slight OCD. I'm not speaking out of turn here, as you know. I bring the humour. And we needed a sense of humour with this case.'

The core team of DCs Conway and Graham, and DI Jed Pidd, was now in place. Pidd delivers what you would expect from a police detective: cropped hair, broad shoulders and a busted nose. He may look like Gene Hunt from *Life on Mars* but his talk is peppered with words like 'healing' and 'closure'.

'Officers don't come into this unit fresh out of training college,' Pidd told me. 'People who come into these units go through a comprehensive selection process and they're generally more mature, more experienced officers. We are used to dealing with people in emotional turmoil. You won't come here to tell a story of historical abuse without having thought about it very, very seriously and been in two minds as to whether you're doing the right thing, because you'll have lived with it for years and years. We're about enabling people to come forward and that's about having the right officers, the right environment. It involves keeping people informed about what's going on and being honest about the prospects of success. It involves taking you on a journey from making a complaint and going to court to getting a conviction. Victims are treated as grown-ups because they are grown-ups but we're asking them about experiences that happened to them when they were children, so there's a bit of mental juggling going on – because we're going to and from the past, scenarios that happened thirty or more years ago.'

By now, Morris had stepped down from his position at Holy Angels and was on bail. Meanwhile, Doctor Boy had given the police names of three other pupils he thought would be able to help with the case. DI Pidd was struck by a particular phrase that he used in his statement: 'extra lessons'.

These two words, though the officer only had a vague suspicion of it at the time, would prove to be the key to unlocking the memories of dozens more ex-pupils.

'When you hear things like that, alarm bells begin to ring,' Pidd explains. 'When there are provisions made for "extra lessons", what that means is lessons that are not, in the view of other pupils, extra attention – in this case, in a storage room at the back of a chemistry lab, where sexual offending can take place. Not only was there the motivation, there was the possibility of accessing children and the opportunity to abuse.'

Pidd decided to release just a little information about the case to see what reaction it generated. On 5 December 2012 an article appeared in the *Manchester Evening News* under the headline POLICE LAUNCH CHILD SEX ABUSE PROBE AT TOP ALL-BOYS SCHOOL NEAR ALTRINCHAM.

No names were mentioned in the piece but there was enough information for any ex-pupil to realise immediately it was Alan Morris that the police were investigating. The article talked about a sixty-three-year-old ex-teacher, now a 'church minister', who had been arrested over incidents dating back over a thirty-year period, including one where a boy was offered 'extra lessons'.

The Shrewsbury Diocese released a statement confirming

that 'a complaint has been received concerning a member of the clergy. [The diocese] is co-operating fully with the statutory agencies involved and the appropriate safeguarding procedures are being followed. The diocese is unable to comment further for legal reasons.'

The school also released a carefully worded statement: 'St Ambrose is deeply concerned about the allegations. We are co-operating fully with the police investigation and welcome the press exposure but cannot comment further at this stage.'

Detectives were by now dealing directly with the school. Things had certainly changed since my day. Apart from Woodeaves – the Christian Brothers' house used originally as classrooms – nothing of the old school physically remained. There had been a £24 million rebuild on the site. The wooden-hut prep classrooms and secondary-school buildings, including the chemistry lab and the Dark Room, had all gone.

'We made the school aware right from the start that the investigation was ongoing and we would need school records,' says DC Conway, 'looking at that evidence as well as the witness evidence. But there were only limited school records – some were burned in the fire at Woodeaves in the 1980s. The school was demolished and rebuilt and, during the transfer to the new school, some were destroyed. Some were sent over to the Christian Brothers in Dublin. You're trying to put the case together, so you're looking at school records to see if there is anything that would support it.'

Officers spoke to the current headmaster, Michael Thompson, and to a teacher who was a contemporary of Alan Morris and who was still at the school. The police thought that this teacher might be able to provide vital information about Morris, as he was a key link to the past and had even shared an office with him.

'He was spoken to at the start of the investigation,' admits Barry Conway. 'What he had to tell us was pretty limited. He said he couldn't assist us and he didn't know anything about what Morris was up to or what was going on.'

In fact there was another current Ambrose teacher who had also worked alongside Alan Morris and was still on staff at the school, but it was some time before police were told about this potentially important source of information: 'We weren't aware of him at the start of the investigation,' admits Barry Conway.

The school then contacted the St Ambrose Old Boys' Association, which holds annual dinners for ex-pupils that are attended by some teachers (though not Alan Morris).

'Between Alan Morris's arrest and trial, the SAOBA maintained a neutral stance,' chairman John Kennedy told me. 'The association did not take action or organise any support for him. We had a message from the college advising us that we should not discuss the case – especially with journalists. We have followed this advice. I attended the college during the 1970s and recall corporal punishment being part of the make-up of the college and, perhaps, the times we lived in. However, I was not, at the time, aware of the charges subsequently levelled at Alan Morris and, strangely, throughout my years as a governor and almost twenty years as Chairman of the Old Boys' Association, no one has ever commented to me or, indeed, any member of the committee about Alan Morris's behaviour. You may find that hard to believe but I can assure you it is absolutely true. We were all shocked, hurt, let down and angry when this all came to light but are also concerned about the impact on current staff and pupils, as I'm sure you can appreciate.'

Meanwhile, the *Manchester Evening News* article was paying dividends. Calls from former pupils began to pour in. It was vital that officers taking calls didn't ask any leading questions that could be highlighted if the case went to court.

'What you do at that initial stage is vital,' confirms DC Barry Conway. 'That is the most important part. Because that impacts so much when you get to trial, that initial contact with witnesses coming forward is so important. Every officer was briefed in terms of: "This is what we will do and this is how we are going to do it. No matter what they ask, this is how we will do it."'

'That article caused a huge amount of telephone calls to the unit from ex-pupils who had either been physically and/ or sexually abused by Alan Morris,' observes DC Nicola Graham. 'We got extra staff in to take the calls and review them. We spoke to and interviewed everybody who came forward. Everyone who wanted to be interviewed was videoed or they provided a statement.'

The calls came in thick and fast, not just from lads who still lived locally but from around the country. Old Ambrosians had travelled far and wide but many kept up to speed with events in Altrincham via the Internet. Eleven years earlier, when Ground Zero had come forward to tell police about what happened to him, he'd rung other ex-pupils to ask them to back up his story. They'd said no. This time, following Doctor Boy's statement, the lads came through.

'I suppose it takes you until you're in your forties or fifties to think that you're ballsy enough, that you've got enough life experience or courage to do something about it,' Doctor Boy told me. 'This is what they say about abused people, they run away from it. I ran away from it for twenty years.'

For ex-pupil Mike Bishop, memories of what had happened to him, and his mum's complaint to the school, were already triggered by ongoing coverage of historical cases involving celebrities in the media. Then he spotted news of the St Ambrose arrest.

'Before this kicked off, I sent my mum a text after the Jimmy Savile stuff had broken. It said, "I can't thank you enough for what you did for me, back when I came to you about Morris." She said, "Don't worry, that's what I'm here to do." About two to three weeks later, I phoned the police and said, "Look, I've got to tell you something." I told them… and this whole journey started.'

Nervous Boy, the lad so stressed by school that he'd pulled his hair out, was tipped off about the investigation by a family member.

'My sister told me. She said, "I know you've got a problem with Alan Morris, you might want to know he's been suspended from his duties, it was announced at the Holy Angels' mass this Sunday." The police then said that if anyone wanted to come forward with any information, they should do so. Like a shot, I was there. "Right, I'm going to get my coat!" My wife was saying, "Stop, think about this," and I said, "No, I'm literally going now! I'm just going down there straight away!" My heart was racing. I rang the police and I remember thinking, *Calm down, do this properly, don't just turn up on the doorstep, do this more slowly.* It was quite surreal. I felt like I was watching myself in some sort of film almost. I've never had to ring the police in my life before.'

Not everyone was quite so keen to speak to the detectives as Nervous Boy. Scott Morgan, who Morris had targeted nearly every day at St Ambrose, was decidedly unsure about the whole thing.

'I had no interest in digging it all up in any way, shape or form,' he told me. 'I didn't want to go to court. I didn't want it associated with my dad. My sister rang the police and, unfortunately, I had to go in and see them. I said, "Under no circumstances do I want to be put into the trial. My dad's nearly seventy, I don't want him worrying about all this stuff." Six months later they rang me and said, "Sorry, you're going on the witness stand." That's when I thought, *You know what, who cares anymore? You might get closure on it all.* You don't. It just brings it all back. It doesn't change who you are.'

From a police point of view Alan Morris was 'boxed off'. He was under bail conditions and not allowed any unsupervised contact with children. He wasn't acting as deacon at the Holy Angels and was no longer a teacher. It meant detectives could concentrate on the testimonies coming from ex-pupils. Recurring themes began to develop: the slow, drawn-out punishments; the inappropriate touching; boys being made to beat each other in the presence of a camera.

Ex-pupil Paul Wills had been involved in an incident at school where he was told to beat a friend of his. By 2012, Wills was living an almost hermit-like existence in a remote part of Scotland; he spotted a mention of a historical case online.

'The word Ambrose caught my eye,' he told me. 'As soon as I saw it, I knew – there was a historical complaint and they wanted information. It was very straightforward. I phoned my friend [Derek Scanlan] and said, "I don't know what you're doing, I don't want to drop you in it but I'm going to tell the police whatever I know." He said to go for it. I knew it needed to be done. There was no mention of Morris. But I knew. I *knew*.

'There were several times in the past when I'd thought about it but would the police have taken me seriously? Going to them and saying this guy was groping our arses and getting us to whip each other... they probably wouldn't. If you ever meet Catholics who didn't go to St Ambrose, you end up swapping war stories with each other about the brutality of teachers. The Morris thing always used to come up and people would look at me and say, "Are you serious?" Then you'd think about calling the police but you'd think, *Nah, what's the point?*'

On the run-up to Christmas 2012, DCs Mike Knowles and Mark Kelly were drafted in to help with witness statements as the size of the task in hand became apparent.

'It was a case of going through the lists, working out what we'd got – it became a logistical thing; an organising thing to make sure we hadn't missed anything,' remembers Barry

Conway. 'It's the biggest investigation I've ever dealt with from every perspective.'

Rather than chasing witnesses and victims, the police essentially sat still and let the ex-pupils come to them. But there was one they did have to chase: Ground Zero. He was understandably angry about what had happened eleven years earlier.

'I think that, in terms of how we look at historical-abuse cases,' reflects DI Pidd, '2001 was a long time ago. But when you get a single allegation made against a man of previous good character, it's actually quite difficult to prove. What we had here [in 2012] was many, many, many individuals coming forward, all saying the same thing. And that was the difference. In these kinds of historical-abuse cases in institutional settings, you're never alone as a victim. It's the sheer weight of numbers that proves the case.'

'That was one of the tricky enquiries really,' admits Barry Conway of Ground Zero. 'We didn't know how he was going to react to us. I know from reading the reports back in 2001 that he was disappointed with the outcome and a bit upset with the way things went. That was one that had to be dealt with sensitively because we really wanted him to be involved in the case.'

The detectives did, indeed, track Ground Zero down and went round to his new address. They were in plain clothes and weren't allowed to identify themselves as police officers, fearful of alerting anyone to the nature of their investigation and identifying Ground Zero as an abuse victim, so they left a message for him.

After all he'd been through, Ground Zero was, by now, a touch paranoid; he promptly changed his phone number and personal details, including his bank account, worried that someone was out to get him. Ex-Ambrose lads can be a bit jumpy.

Eventually, the police managed to persuade him they meant no harm and to come back into the fold. 'Once we had the first meeting with him, it was great from there and he came on board,' says DC Conway. 'He did a great job in court as well – that was one of the many plus points.'

Meanwhile, back at Rivington Road, sitting quietly in the upstairs room he used as an office, Alan Morris was oblivious to the sheer amount of work going on a couple of miles away. But he must have known that the carefully constructed facade he'd maintained since the early 1970s was finally beginning to crumble.

As the evidence mounted, other old boys began to come forward to talk about their time at St Ambrose. However, some of them didn't want to talk about Alan Morris but about other teachers at the school. And some of the experiences they wanted to share would prove even more shocking.

CHAPTER SIX

THE LOST BOYS

The investigation into Alan Morris was, by this stage, opening up a lot of boxes for a lot of ex-pupils. They came to the police with their stories about life under the St Ambrose regime; some of their experiences stretched back to the 1960s and involved members of staff other than Morris. The names of one teacher and a Christian Brother would crop up again and again.

The officers investigating St Ambrose would eventually spend as much, if not more, time speaking to some of these men as they would with the pupils affected by Morris. To me, these ex-pupils seemed like ghosts, floating on the edges of the investigation; hovering; waiting. Some would post cryptic messages on website forums by now buzzing with comment on the case. Later, a few could be seen in the public gallery during the trial. They seemed to be looking for something, yet they were unlikely to ever truly find it – so myself and the police called them the 'Lost Boys'.

Some were lads who had suffered at the hands of a teacher now out of reach of the police – because he was dead. The earliest allegation of inappropriate touching by a lay teacher dated back to the early 1960s.

Despite knowing that the person they were accusing was no longer around to face the consequences, the Lost Boys still came forward to share what they knew. It helped the investigation, giving officers a wider view of what went on at the school. More importantly, it helped the victims themselves. Middle-aged men tend to be a bit queasy about words like 'closure' but that, it seems, is what these ex-pupils were looking for.

'There wasn't just Alan Morris,' confirms DC Nicola Graham. 'Allegations were made against other people – Christian Brothers and teachers – of physical and sexual abuse. Unfortunately, these people had all passed away. But because it was our investigation, there's a duty of care towards those people. Anyone who wanted to be was interviewed to give their version of events, to give them some sort of closure, so they know they've been believed.'

It appeared that Morris was the last (as far as we're aware) of a line of abusers at St Ambrose. 'Alan Morris was by no means alone,' says DI Jed Pidd, echoing the opinion of his colleague. 'He's singular in that he's *alive*. At that time, there was clearly a culture of physical and sexual abuse of young, vulnerable children at the school for years. Obviously, there's very little we can do when the person is dead. However, the process of healing is, perhaps, started by people telling the truth to the authorities about what happened – and that story being taken seriously, listened to and acted upon.'

The stories of the other ex-pupils chiefly involved two teachers: Brother Edward Ignatius Baylor and Norman 'Sam' Wilkinson. The following is the testimony of one ex-pupil, recorded by the police along with fourteen others relating to crimes beyond the incidents involving Alan Morris.

Simon O'Brien was a boy I knew well at school. He'd started at St Ambrose prep a year before me in 1971. I hadn't seen him for nearly thirty-five years when we sat on a bench in the grounds of a church one day, in the summer of 2014. This is what he told me:

'The prep school at St Ambrose was fee paying and my mother worked extra hard to scrape the money together. We didn't have much money at all. At the age of seven I found myself in prep one. I was overawed by it, the mystique and the smell of it. From day one I felt under huge pressure to succeed because of the extra work my mother was doing to get the fees together. I knew I had to do well and that thought didn't leave me until the back end of fifth year in the big school.

'The Christian Brothers – these guys dressed in black – from day one, I thought they were a bit strange. Not least because on the third day I was there I was swinging on a desk with another lad and I got the strap. That was a bit of a reality check. *Whoah!* This school's different. These guys are religious but they're nasty bastards. The straps they used on you and I were barber's strops, used for sharpening the old-fashioned cutthroat blades. They got them from a barber's shop in Altrincham, the same place I went to get my hair cut. They used to dangle down next to the sinks. When I went in there, my mother would ask me why I was shaking. It was because I related the strops at the barber's to the straps at St Ambrose.

'I got picked on by pretty much every teacher. It was like they were in cahoots with one another: lots of punishments, lots of pressure, lots of... why me? Then there was the other thing, which was shocking and soul destroying.

'I was sexually abused by Brother Baylor. That started not long after I got to the school. He was balding, had a comb-over, yellow teeth, a slight Irish accent. He taught sports. I had an immaculate sports kit – nice, pressed, white shorts and football top. We had kit inspections and Brother Baylor would pick out the best-dressed boys. He'd detain those boys in a horrible changing room. I can tell you the colour of the tiles, the damp smell. Everything. The rest of the lads would file out to play football and I'd be left with three or four others. I guess we were being eyed up – the sweet, innocent, well-dressed little boys – so he could have his evil way.

'I was generally at the start of the queue. Maybe I looked nicer than the others. He'd lead me to the communal bath area and on the floor there was a double mattress – an off-white, stained, horrible, stripy mattress. He'd get me to lie face down and he would lie on top of me with my legs apart. He'd start tickling me. I'd wriggle around and that was the start of the stimulation for him. I'd feel fumbling between my legs and he'd get his penis out. Then I'd feel something warm as he'd put it between the flesh of my thighs. I didn't know what this was. He'd tickle me more and I'd wriggle more. His beard would be right next to my face. His breath was foul. He smelled of whisky. He would mutter under his breath.

'Sometimes he would lean back in, God forbid, a sort of doggy position. I didn't know what this was. I could see the end of his knob between my legs while he was tickling me. It was then that I realised this was not right. He'd lay me back down, reach round and start masturbating me. I hadn't a clue what this was about. I felt something wet down there and I guess he'd ejaculated. He did it when he was in his cassock. I'd turn round and see him zip himself up and put his sports kit on.

'This would take about twenty minutes. The double whammy was that the other kids would be playing football – I'd come out and I'd be late onto the pitch. So I'd get bent over and be given the slipper for being late. What are you to do? Then you go home and your mother says to you, "Did you have a good day at school? Did you play sport?" I was a bit quiet, a bit withdrawn. It was fucking me over.

'That was during the week. At weekends he'd say there was a football match on and could I play, because I was such a good sportsman. My father would take me into school. I'd look around for the other boys... but they weren't there. There was no game. He'd say, "While you're here, let me have a look at your sports kit." And down we'd go. Then he'd ring my father and say, "There wasn't a game, my mistake, can you come and pick your son up?" It was very targeted. This went on pretty much throughout the whole of prep one, until I moved up to prep two. I can only imagine that he did the same to the new prep ones.

'I felt thoroughly dirty. Why didn't I tell anybody? I was frightened. Scared. Embarrassed. [It was] fear of retribution. Fear of not being believed. There was no room for me to confide that kind of information to my parents. They were too busy beating the shit out of each other in their violent marriage. I knew I had to deal with it, so each time I put it into a "box". I had nowhere to go. There was nobody I could talk to. I dealt with all my problems myself. My father came from a strict Victorian-style upbringing. God knows what would have happened if I'd have told him. So you bottle it.

'It put a nail in the coffin of any education I might get at the school. Not a chance. Every time there was a test or an exam I'd be back in that changing room. I couldn't concentrate. I'd started to fail already. There had been a black hole blown inside me.'

Those are truly terrible words: a *black hole* inside a little boy of seven or eight. It's apparent that Brother Baylor had implanted such dark voids inside many other boys too. Baylor seems to have been shunted from school to school, ricocheting around the Christian Brothers' system for decades.

'Baylor is known to have taught in Christian Brother schools throughout the northwest of England, as well as in Leeds, Edinburgh, Stoke and Gibraltar,' DI Pidd confirmed to me. 'A further eleven boys have come forward, all complaining of indecent assaults involving Baylor. This offending again involved a significantly similar *modus operandi* that I know your contacts have told you about and, therefore, given that eleven boys have come forward, a further eleven crimes are recorded as detected on our systems. In my view, it is inevitable that, given the overwhelming evidence, charges would have followed if Baylor were alive. Baylor, in fact, died in 1992, in a care home in Dublin.'

Another pupil also contacted me about Brother Baylor. Richard Eames had a similar tale to tell about the sports teacher. He even drew me a map of the school, showing the classrooms, the changing rooms and the position where Baylor would put the mattress on the floor.

Eames had attended St Ambrose College from 1964–69. He was a little older than the other boys, as he repeated prep three because he'd been in hospital.

'Brother Baylor was the games master,' he told me. 'The abuse started in 1969, when I was eleven or twelve years old. I was neither good at games nor keen on sports. I was myopic and had recent scars from hospital operations. I was slow getting changed into sports kit and somehow Brother Baylor contrived that we would be alone together in the changing rooms, while the other children had either gone on to the pitch or back to their class. He'd say, "I'll have to give you a warm-up because you're not that brilliant at sports. You need to warm up." He produced a mattress from somewhere and placed it in the middle of the changing room. He then told me to lie on it and he started tickling me. He'd be muttering some sort of rubbish while he did it. He'd make encouraging noises as if it were a game on the sports pitch. I was lying helpless on the ground. He had his arms on me. I was incapacitated. Then he'd say, "Off you go to cross-country," as if it were the most normal thing in the world. This happened on probably less than half a dozen occasions. Although I didn't suspect anything sinister, I did think it odd enough to mention to my parents. They seemed to have a moment's concern but then dismissed it.

'My mother was a stalwart of the school Christmas and summer fairs, baking cakes for sale and having me deliver an extra, free supply of her renowned meringues to the brothers' house. Brother Baylor had so won her confidence that, when he suggested taking me and two other boys on a holiday to London, she raised no objection. I'd never been away from home except for holidays with my parents.

'So in the summer of 1970, the four of us got on a train to London. When we got there, he told us some story about the hotel being double-booked and tried to get us into the YMCA instead. They refused and we ended up at another B&B. We drew lots to share the two rooms. One of the other boys got Baylor. I don't know what happened in Baylor's room because the boy never talked about it, although I knew him all through school and met him again in the 1980s. The only odd thing that happened on that holiday was when Baylor brought the other boy into our room and got him to massage oil into my body, while he looked on. The only other experience I had with Baylor was during cross-country. I had tried, clumsily, to climb a metal fence and thought that I might have cut my groin. I naïvely mentioned this to Baylor, whose response was to plunge his hand down my shorts. After a bit of a feel, he pronounced everything all right and I marvelled at his medical knowledge, being able to make a diagnosis just by feel without even looking.'

Meanwhile, Simon O'Brien had moved up to the secondary

school, where he came across the charismatic and apparently kind drama and biology teacher, Sam Wilkinson. O'Brien, who had been abused by Brother Baylor in the prep, was also having a torturous time at home. When Wilkinson offered him a role making props for the drama department, for the first time in years he felt safe.

'He took me under his wing,' Simon told me. 'I thought, *He's a good teacher, he's kind and he has a laugh with us.* I was feeling pretty vulnerable by that stage – I felt I could trust him. I didn't see anything sinister in Sam. I know now there probably was.

'Every second Sunday I would go to his house and clean his car for two quid. At the end he'd say, "Come on in," and he'd give me beer. He bought me a Watney's Red Barrel Party Four. He'd give me cigarettes. I'd sit in his lounge. It was all very comfortable. I was about fourteen. He'd listen to my stories – all of a sudden, I had someone to talk to about how shit it was at home. He'd get me to do odd jobs around the house, climb ladders and he'd always be below me, looking up. It seemed innocent at the time but I know exactly what he was doing now.

'At the end of a project, he would invite us and the parents round to celebrate. He befriended them. I got quite drunk once because it was normal for me to drink his beer. My dad said, "What are you doing drinking that?" I said, "Sam gives me this all the time."

'We made a film – a ghost story at his house. David, you were in it too! Remember the clothes we had to wear? Leather shorts, lederhosen and knee socks. He would help me on with my socks. The shorts were loose fitting so there was plenty of room to get a hand in there – which he did. As he pulled my socks up, his hand would continue up the thigh and grab a hold of my meat and two veg. And linger. I remember saying, "What the fuck have you just done, Sam?" He said, "I can't resist a male thigh." He was a thigh man.'

'Had Wilkinson been alive today, he would have faced charges of indecent assault against four different boys at St Ambrose,' says Di Pidd.

To me and many other boys who counted Sam Wilkinson as a friend during their time at St Ambrose, these are terribly sad words to hear. For many, myself included, Sam had been more than a teacher; he'd been our ally. Many lads who'd been happy to talk to me about Alan Morris shut down when it came to Wilkinson because they felt a sense of loyalty to him. But the reality was that, while Morris used fear to abuse boys at the school, Wilkinson used a mixture of charm and alcohol to get what he wanted.

'Evidence has been gathered from these victims [of Baylor and Wilkinson] using exactly the same process as for the Morris prosecutions,' confirmed DI Jed Pidd. 'These crimes are recorded as "detected" under a Home Office Counting Rules [HOCR] procedure where, had the suspect been alive, there would be sufficient evidence to charge. In my view, given the separate boys that have come forward as complainants and the similarity of *modus operandi*, charges would have been inevitable had Wilkinson and Baylor been alive.'

Looking back on those days, it seems the whole experience of St Ambrose became too much for Simon O'Brien. By the age of sixteen, he seemed drained.

'I remember going into the gym to sit my O-levels. I worked so hard to revise but I was an absolute, utter wreck. Then all of a sudden, I wasn't at school. I just disappeared. I don't remember leaving. I remember coming home with my results: one grade C in geography. I was petrified. It was like a vacuum. I remember thinking, *What the fuck just happened there?*'

Like many lads, O'Brien went to college to try to make up for lost time – and thrived. He's now a pilot in the RAF. But the memories of his childhood were hidden away and never spoken of.

'It was all put in a box on the last day of school and it came out on 15 January 2013,' he explained. 'I was abroad and got an email from my mother to say she'd been in touch with a policeman from Altrincham police station who was investigating an allegation of abuse involving a teacher at the senior school at St Ambrose. No names, no details. As I read the email. I saw "St Ambrose"... and "abuse". I rang the police and said I needed to speak to someone about similar incidents. I started to tell them... I got ten seconds into it and utterly broke down. I found it difficult to breathe and my mouth wasn't working fast enough. My brain was pushing this stuff out, to the extent that I had to slam the phone down. I rang again and apologised. It set off other explosions. It rattled other padlocks on other boxes. This box of bad memories had started to shake. I'd kept it under lock and key for forty-odd years. I realised it was going to come out and, boy, did it come out.'

Fifteen ex-pupils, including Simon, gave statements about what happened to them at St Ambrose. The incidents were logged as crimes but all those concerned knew that they could be taken no further. But at least someone had listened.

'I'd like to think they've been treated sympathetically, with care, with kindness and with dignity,' says DI Jed Pidd. 'We've listened to what they had to say and we've believed them. It's clear they've been horrendously abused. You can only feel very, very sorry for them.'

Officers from the Altrincham team – people of a similar generation to the St Ambrose lads – were also shocked by the stories of everyday life at St Ambrose. The sexual abuse was clearly disturbing but the ways in which boys were punished on a more mundane level also struck them as bizarre.

They came across 'totally inappropriate ways of dealing with things', according to DC Barry Conway. 'Some of the things they told us… I think sometimes that, if you told people, they wouldn't believe some of the stories that have been told to us, on top of everything with Alan Morris.'

Here's one such memory shared with DC Conway: 'There was a young boy who got a scholarship at the school – he wasn't from the richest of families and Mum and Dad couldn't afford the uniform. Because he didn't have the right uniform, he got bullied by the teachers and prefects and was made to wear a female uniform from the nearby Loreto girls' school. He had to walk round in a dress for weeks and weeks until he got the correct uniform. There were lots of examples of that type of thing.'

Indeed, here's one more: 'Another anecdote related to a swimming gala where a pupil had a heart attack and died in the pool,' DC Conway said. 'I was told that a friend of the young boy who died was in assembly the following day and broke down crying. He was taken in front of the school and beaten with the strap by the headteacher for crying. So when you hear something like that, it becomes hard to believe... but I'm not doubting anything that witness said.'

CHAPTER SEVEN

MY LIFE HIT
THE BUFFERS

Many of the lads who came forward in the St Ambrose investigation were invited to various police stations around the country, to give videotaped evidence. I went to give mine at Hazel Grove, Stockport, in December 2012.

The address I was given didn't look like a police station at all but more like a house. That was the idea. It was a place where people could give evidence without feeling intimidated.

The video suites had the look of a doctor's waiting room: a couple of boxy brown seats and a sofa, some low-key framed pictures on the wall. But there was one aspect I found puzzling – like many a doctor's waiting room, there was a box of toys in the corner. In fact, I found the presence of the toys rather chilling. It took me a while to realise that these 'visual interview suites' were not just the preserve of fifty-year-old blokes talking about what happened to them as kids.

'We have toys because we interview a lot of children and sometimes we need a distraction,' explains DC Nicola Graham. 'We have pens, paper and colouring books too; aids to get the best evidence. Years ago, we'd just take a child into a police station and do a question-and-answer session. Now we get much better evidence. We're the Child Protection Investigation Unit – so we interview children as young as four but we can also interview a bloke of fifty or an old-age pensioner of ninety.

'About 50 per cent of our work involves speaking to children. We interview vulnerable and intimidated witnesses – children, vulnerable adults, victims or witnesses to crimes of a sexual nature. It's called an ABE interview: "achieving best evidence" by a visual interview. The integrity of the evidence is paramount – there's a set format, there's no prompting and you've got to be specially trained to get the most out of the person you're interviewing: lots of open-ended questions, no leading questions. The starting point of any investigation is the testimony of the victims. You build a case from witnesses, recent complainants, stuff you find at the scene, school records, but you can't have an investigation without witnesses coming to speak to us.

'It's still intimidating. I'm going to ask you to tell me about your experiences at the hands of Alan Morris and, if that's sexual, it's a very difficult thing to talk about. We're asking people we don't know to tell us about what is probably their first sexual experience. Everyone reacts differently. We have plenty of tissues in here because people are telling you stuff that's caused them a lot of grief over the years. They're human beings and they get upset when they talk about traumas.'

At this stage, I thought I was at the Hazel Grove unit to help provide background information to the case. I didn't think for a moment that I'd be classed as a victim. But it appeared that, because of the sexual element of the beatings, I *was*.

In the video suite, I went through the three aspects I thought would help: the violent regime of the school and the culture of beatings; how Morris had threatened us by saying he'd 'take the teeth' of any boy who spoke about him; and my dealings with him, describing him as a psychological as well as physical bully.

'Of all the teachers who used corporal punishment, there was only one who was clearly savouring it, enjoying it, ritualising it – that teacher was Alan Morris,' my statement read. 'It was explicit and clear to even the youngest of pupils what the deal was with Morris. It was not schoolyard tittle-tattle or gossip, it was information you needed to know about Morris and how to stay out of his way. You avoided going for extra lessons at lunchtime with him. The rest of the teachers were just violent bastards but Morris was different because he sexualised the ritual of punishment.'

'You can't lead them,' says DC Conway about the statement process. 'The whole point of video-recording a witness testimony is that it's a transparent and open process. There's a time code on it, you can see me and see the witness [on the video]. You can't put words in people's mouths, you can't ask leading questions, we have to take them through it bit by bit and summarise. But you're not dealing with something that happened yesterday or last week; it's something that happened twenty or thirty years ago and that is the problem that you've got. Because you're not going to remember everything – it's impossible – and, if you did, there would be something drastically wrong.'

My statement continued, 'With regards to Morris and the sexualised element to his behaviour, there was a lot of sexual innuendo in his lessons. When you had to bend down for his punishments, it was always done gently, how he lifted your blazer vent up to make sure everything was in the right place. He would place his hands on your backside to make sure everything was in the right place. He would push you in the back to make sure you bent over properly. I never spoke to anyone about my experiences at the school because I thought it was a privilege to be at the school and my mum had worked very hard to get me there and I didn't want to cause any trouble.'

Through statements like mine and those of the other lads coming forward, detectives were building up a picture of what life was like at St Ambrose during Morris's time.

'Obviously the main theme with Morris was this cloak of discipline that he used to abuse boys,' Barry Conway told me. 'So you had the scenario where he would get boys to spank each other and where he'd get a pupil on his knee and smack their bottoms, put his hand on their bottoms and touch their genitals – this general inappropriate use of corporal punishment. Plus there were the kind of rituals that he would use; I think that was a big thing that came through. It wasn't a quick grope: it was a long ritual of build-up, almost a theatrical scenario. I think that is where it becomes horrendous, especially for people who had to do it repeatedly on a daily, monthly, yearly basis. The prospect of knowing what's going to come and knowing it's not going to be a quick thing but a long, drawn-out scenario. That ritual makes it horrific: a massive psychological power thing. I think there are all kinds of dynamics going on. The very real impression that I got when we were dealing with the witnesses was that some were still frightened of him. Even now, they were still frightened of him.'

DC Conway personally carried out twenty interviews with ex-pupils and a pattern soon became glaringly obvious: the regime of violence at St Ambrose; the Dark Room; the beatings; the touching; getting boys to beat each other, or even beat themselves; the photographs – these were the recurrent themes of the testimonies.

'It was basically like *Groundhog Day*,' he told me. 'Because what the people were telling us was repeated and sometimes you knew what they were going to say before they said it. Once you got into double figures of speaking to people, you knew what was going to happen next.'

The detectives travelled far and wide to interview the lads – but one ex-pupil was deemed a little too far off their beat. Derek Scanlan, who had been involved in one of the incidents when boys were told to cane each other, now lived on the island of Lewis and Harris in the Outer Hebrides.

'Barry Conway was quite keen to interview me but, for some reason, he wasn't allowed to,' Scanlan told me. 'They sent a request to Stornoway police. I went in and gave a statement. It was a strange thing to cast your mind back all those years. The statement took me four hours. I was happy to do it – the only way to move forward is to address these issues. All the time you questioned yourself: *Am I making too much of what happened?* Then you think, *If someone treated my kids like this, what would I do? How on earth would I behave?* They would come straight home and tell me because we have that kind of relationship, not like relationships we had years ago. I probably wouldn't be calling the police, put it that way.'

As the police contacted the last of the lads to come forward, some of the ex-pupils made contacts of their own. In early 2013 some of the victims approached legal firms, including Slater & Gordon, a Manchester-based company better known by their previous name, Pannone. They wanted to know about the possibility of compensation after the case concluded – a subject that would divide many of those involved.

Mollie Whittall, an assistant solicitor at Slater & Gordon who deals exclusively with historical-abuse cases, coordinated the requests. 'When we were first contacted by ex-pupils, the police investigation was ongoing,' she told me. 'Obviously, we didn't want to interfere with that investigation and we told people, "If you haven't spoken to the police yet, you need to do so." Nothing's going to happen until the police investigation is over.'

It turned out that the Christian Brothers had taken out insurance against claims of sex abuse decades earlier; as the brothers ran St Ambrose, if the compensation claims were successful, their insurance would potentially pay out claims made by victims of Alan Morris.

'The Catholic Church has always maintained that, if you go back to the 1960s and 1970s, there wasn't the institutional knowledge and understanding of sex abuse,' explains Richard

Scorer, Slater & Gordon's head of injury and negligence. 'But that is contradicted by the fact that they took out insurance against those very liabilities. Some of them were taking out insurance against this kind of thing going back to the 1960s.'

The company is fully aware of the unease that seeking compensation for abuse creates and of the 'ambulance-chaser' reputation that labels firms like theirs.

'Generally, there is a perception about that whole compensation-culture thing and that's frustrating because we think we're doing a really good job and it's important to us,' says Whittall. 'That perception is something we have to deal with. We don't approach people, people come to us. People may have seen the case discussed on a blog or know someone we're dealing with already. St Ambrose is local too.'

'We're in the public eye a lot,' confirms Scorer, 'particularly with abuse cases and particularly around some of the Operation Yewtree cases – Jimmy Savile, Rolf Harris, Max Clifford and so on. We've also dealt with a lot of litigation over the years involving the Catholic Church.'

Slater & Gordon realised early on that the allegations were typical of church-run institutions but the nature of the victims was unusual. 'It was obvious they were very serious about the allegations being made,' says Mollie Whittall. 'It definitely seemed like the kind of abuse we'd seen before at this type of school. This case stands out because Morris was at the school for nearly twenty years – but also, because of the nature of the school, the majority of people who've come forward have been professional people, people with good jobs, backgrounds where you wouldn't necessarily expect this to have happened.'

Slater & Gordon told me there was only so much information they could reveal about the progress of the claims, because of client confidentiality – so I signed up as a client. Problem solved; though the thought of any money resulting from it made me feel distinctly uneasy.

Meanwhile, as the number of ex-pupils who'd come forward headed towards the fifty mark, detectives were at the stage where they needed to re-interview the man at the centre of the investigation. Officers now had multiple complaints of indecent assault and gross indecency with children to put to Alan Morris, as well as questions about the material they'd found on his computer and DVDs.

Morris was brought back to Pendleton police station on Thursday, 11 April 2013, for a marathon interview session with DCs Barry Conway and Nicola Graham.

'He was rearrested in relation to indecent assaults and gross indecency with children, basically on the strength of what people had told us,' explains DC Conway. 'We started at 10.45am and finished at 6.45pm. There was a lot of evidence. There were fifty witness testimonies to go through, as well as the computer evidence, and then challenging him on these inconsistencies from the interview about the pornography.'

Morris was accompanied that day by solicitor Judith Hawkins from legal firm Rhys Vaughan. Once the usual checks and cautions were dealt with, Morris was told that the police wanted to go through the allegations of 'suspected sexual touching of children' and to give him the opportunity to respond to them.

DC Conway: During your time as a teacher at St Ambrose College, did you indecently assault pupils, either by touching them sexually on their genitals or bottom?

Morris: No.

DC Conway: During your time as a teacher at St Ambrose College, did you perform sexual acts on yourself in the presence of pupils?

Morris: No.

DC Conway: During your time as a teacher at St Ambrose College, did you perform sexual acts of punishment and discipline on pupils for your own sexual pleasure?

Morris: No.

DC Conway: Do you have a sexual interest in sadomasochistic practices, which includes the scenario of teacher on pupil?

Morris: No, no.

DC Conway: Speaking again specifically on the scenario of teacher on pupil, is that a sexual interest of yours?

Morris: No.

DC Conway: During your time at St Ambrose College, did you incite pupils to perform acts on each other, i.e. spanking themselves for your own sexual pleasure?

Morris: The second part of the sentence is the one that I'm going to say no to.

DC Conway: Did you get pupils at St Ambrose to spank themselves?

Morris: One of the things that I did was to, for example – if two boys had been fighting, I would say to them, 'Now, you know, here are you fighting, you are going to have to, you know, correct each other.' It was always in a very minor key, never even remotely more than gentle, and I said, 'That's what will happen to you if, you know, you're fighting again.' But I said, 'Since you are both fighting each other, you might as well chastise each other.'

DC Conway: So you did get pupils to chastise each other?

Morris: In... gently, yes, gently.

DC Conway: But to the second part, which is did you do it for your sexual pleasure?

Morris: No, no, no, it was a way of trying to stop them doing whatever naughty things they were doing without actually, you know, being, erm... vocal to them or distressing them.

DC Conway: So it was for their benefit?

Morris: Yes, it was for their benefit, to stop them. I mean, you know, you're always [dealing] every day with, like, naughtiness that could easily end up in harm, so, if they were fighting together, I said, 'Now you will have to chastise each other, rather than me chastising you,' and it was always, I think... I thought it was always received humorously and, at the end of it, I would say, 'Now go away and don't do it again.'

DC Conway: During your time at St Ambrose College, did you perform a sexual act, i.e. masturbate in front of a child in a public place?

Morris: No.

DC Conway: During your time at St Ambrose College, did you take indecent photographs of children under the age of sixteen and, by that, I mean taking photographs

of pupils' bottoms and positioning them in provocative poses for your own sexual pleasure?
Morris: No.

Alan Morris seemed to treat the allegations – and the officers who were putting them to him – as beneath him. 'A very arrogant man who has never shown any remorse,' describes DC Nicola Graham. 'He lives in a different world to us. Very arrogant.'

The high-handed manner in which he dealt with pupils at St Ambrose had not dimmed over the years. 'I'm not a psychologist,' says DC Barry Conway. 'And I don't profess to be but many people noted the arrogance of him throughout – a kind of superiority complex. He saw himself as being above me, without any shadow of a doubt, and above anyone else involved in the investigation. But it's just my job, in the interview, to ask the questions. How he reacts to me, what he thinks of me, is irrelevant.'

'I utterly, absolutely and definitively refute any sexual touching, groping of genitals or anything like that,' Morris said during the interviews. 'I [had] long since... I think by... even by the middle of the 1970s decided that it was totally inappropriate to smack people for the poverty of their work because it just was a totally ineffective method. The only way to make them work harder was to make them, in my case, write out notes again, again and again until they got the message. I'm utterly, utterly sick of this [accusation of] groping of genitals and [it] just makes me sick to the pit of my stomach.'

The interviews continued as Morris was asked about each boy's allegations:

DC Conway: The next witness is Paul Wills, who was a pupil at St Ambrose from 1979 through to the time he finished at senior school a number of years after that. Again, do you recall a pupil [named] Paul Wills?

Morris: I don't, I'm afraid, I don't.

DC Conway: Did you teach him at St Ambrose?

Morris: Since I can't remember him, I can't say yes or no to that.

DC Conway: Did you have cause to discipline him?

Morris: Again, since I can't remember him, I can't say yes or no to that.

DC Conway: Did you discipline him with another pupil?

Morris: Again, since I can't remember him, I can't say yes or no to that.

DC Conway: What method of discipline did you use?

Morris: Since I can't remember him, I can't say yes or no to that.

DC Conway: Did you get him to punish another pupil?

Morris: Again, since I can't remember him, I can't say yes or no to that.

DC Conway: Did you touch him sexually?

Morris: No, I never touched anybody sexually, so that I will say no to, even though I can't remember him.

[Further discussion about school discipline follows. DC Conway reads out the account from Paul Wills.]

DC Conway: What have you got to say about that?

Morris: Well, as I said, first of all, I can't remember him at all and so I would reject all of the references to erect penises and groping. Though I cannot remember him or the others, I would utterly reject the erect penis, the groping. Well, I have absolutely no memory of the incident at all.

[General discussion about the school follows. DC Conway recaps.]

DC Conway: You say there was no sexual touching and, if there was any discipline, it wouldn't be for sexual pleasure. Is that correct?

Morris: Correct.

DC Conway: The next witness is Derek Scanlan. What can you tell me about Derek Scanlan? He was a pupil at St Ambrose between 1979 and 1984.

Morris: I can't remember him at all either.

DC Conway: Did you teach that person?

Morris: Again, I can't remember.

DC Conway: Did you discipline that person?

Morris: I can't remember, since I can't remember him.

DC Conway: Did you discipline him with another pupil?

Morris: Again, I can't remember because I can't remember him.

DC Conway: What method was used?

Morris: I can't remember the incident, so I can't answer that question. You keep on bringing up a plimsoll. It was the one thing that I simply couldn't use because I just found it impossible to get my hand round it.

DC Conway: [There are] two witnesses [who] have said

that the plimsoll... they used it on each other. You didn't use it on them? They were hitting each other with the plimsoll? You were not using the plimsoll?

Morris: Well, I can't remember... can't remember at all.

DC Conway: Did you sexually touch Derek Scanlan?

Morris: I cannot... first of all, I say I never sexually touched anybody, although I cannot remember this boy Scanlan.

DC Conway: So, regarding Derek Scanlan's evidence [statement read out], what have you got to say about that?

Morris: Again, though I can't remember the incident, I reject absolutely the groping around the genital area. I just cannot remember those people but I absolutely reject the groping or, indeed, the delight.

Incident after incident, allegation after allegation, was put to Morris, including a statement by a pupil who said Morris forced him to remove his trousers and pants, and to take a beating when he returned to the school to bring back some books. It was claimed Morris had also partially undressed, touching the youth and pushing his penis against the teenager as he hit him.

Alan Morris: That's the best bit of fiction I've heard all day, it is just so outrageously untrue, absolutely... he should be writing novels. If people didn't bring their books back, they were simply charged for the book that they had lost – losing books in school is a major, major, major problem and one just has to charge them for the books they lose in order for us to buy new ones. That is the most sustained and outrageous piece of fiction.

DC Conway also put details of my statement to Morris.

DC Conway: The next person I am going to move onto is a David Nolan, who said he was a pupil at the school between 1972 and 1981. Does David Nolan mean anything to you?

Morris: Again, I think there was more than one Nolan, so I can't remember which would have been David Nolan. [Discussion about other Nolans at the school.] I mean, again, it is not an uncommon [name].

DC Conway: Did you teach somebody called Nolan?

Morris: I certainly taught one of them, one of the Nolans, yes. In fact, I'm not sure that it wasn't in that very naughty class that I mentioned but I can't remember.

DC Conway: Probably looking at mid-1970s through to 1981. That period of time.

Morris: I don't think that was the Nolan.

DC Conway: You can't remember that name, David Nolan?

Morris: I can't remember. I can only remember that I taught some Nolans.

DC Conway: There wasn't anything sexual between yourself and anybody called Nolan?

Morris: No.

DC Conway: David Nolan provided evidence within which he spoke about yourself and your discipline methods and what he described as inappropriate use of corporal punishment, which he believed you obtained sexual gratification from administering. He stated that you used a spatula, which was a kind of flat piece of wood, to hit pupils on their backside. The pupils would be given a choice of extra lessons, which took place in a dark room in the chemistry lab, or being hit in front of the class. David described being hit on the backside by yourself in front of the class. He also described what would occur when he was alone with you. David described what he called a ritual that preceded the punishment, by how you would lift the flap of the back of the blazer and you would feel the backside. From that he said you appeared to be getting sexual gratification. David also described that there were underlying sexual innuendoes from yourself during lessons. He [said you] made threats to all the pupils in a class and said that, if anybody said anything against you, there would be trouble. He recalls the final school report he got from St Ambrose. In the report, he remembers that you wrote down in Latin the term 'The Battle is Over'. [Morris says this in Latin.] So, regarding that last comment, did you do that?

Morris: I had a reputation for writing witty things on reports. Even [on] the university reports.

DC Conway: Do you recall using that particular Latin phrase?

Morris: No but, I mean, I could have done. I also used to if someone was very good – I used to say *magna cum laudi* [with great praise].

DC Conway: So, regarding what David said, what have you got to say regarding that?

Morris: I can't remember him. So it's impossible if you can't remember anybody to say anything... terrible trouble [remembering].

Finally, when the last piece of evidence from the fiftieth pupil was put to Morris, this is how the interview ended:

DC Conway: So that is the end of the witnesses who have provided accounts to the police in the investigation. We had quite a lot of different accounts and different scenarios and different situations. Would there be any reason why these people would make this up against you?

Solicitor: Well, I'm going to advise my client against speculating.

Morris: Well, I'm going to take my solicitor's advice.

It took ten tapes to record Alan Morris's denials of all the evidence that was put to him. After every two or three tapes, he was given a thirty-minute comfort break. As well as the statements of ex-pupils – including my own – being put to him, there was the issue of him apparently lying about the pornography at Rivington Road.

It's at this stage that Morris came up with a story as to why he had recordings of *The Dirty Dean of Discipline* and the like in his possession. It was the kind of excuse a schoolboy might have concocted: 'Oh those? I forgot about those... Anyway, I was just keeping them for a friend...'

Morris told police about this friend: the mysterious Mahjid Mahmood, a man in his early thirties he'd met on one of the online forums he frequented – either *Caffmos* or *Silver Daddies*. Morris said he found this man 'phenomenally erotic' and that the pair would meet up a couple of times a year for sex at Rivington Road. But Mahjid's real interest was sadomasochism and discipline. That, Morris claimed, was why he had the sexual material – as foreplay for his friend. Deacon Morris had no real interest in that sort of thing; it was all for Mahjid's benefit – the material 'threw the switch' for him.

The detectives asked if they could speak to this gentleman to confirm the story. 'Morris said no,' DC Conway recalls. 'He said, "He lives in Birmingham in a very strong Muslim community. He would be in fear of honour-based violence if they found out he was a practising homosexual and his life would be in danger."'

'So we offered to meet him, if Alan Morris arranged a meeting: do it sensitively, away from Birmingham, away from the police station, totally confidential, only two or three people would know about it, meet him, speak to him and see if he'd do us a statement, because that would be the best way forward.'

During the initial search of Rivington Road, Morris's phone was seized and there was, indeed, an 'MM' listed in the contacts. But officers weren't allowed to ring him. It was, literally, Alan Morris's call.

'From an investigation point of view, [if] we're dealing with that aspect of honour-based violence, a mobile-phone number is no good,' Conway explains. 'We can't cold-call somebody as if we're selling a PPI. We don't know who's answering – it could put that person in more danger. We would not do that. We wouldn't do a subscriber check on that number to find out where he lives and send an officer round again for the same reason. So it's not as simple as saying, "You've got a number, ring it." Because, as Morris is saying, potentially, this person's life is in danger if you [make] contact.'

It was a typically elegant excuse – here's a man who can back up my story but you can't call him. By the time the case got to court, Morris's forbidden love for Mahjid Mahmood across the cultural divide would develop into a tale of epic proportions.

With the gruelling second set of interviews over, Alan Morris returned to Rivington Road for a little cold-calling of his own. He started contacting former pupils, asking for help – he wanted people who might speak on his behalf – the more successful or prestigious the better. One ex-pupil, David Lee, was contacted by another former Ambrosian on Morris's behalf. Lee then received the following email:

Dear David,

You may well be aware that I left teaching some eighteen years ago through ill health and that for the last twenty years I've been the ordained deacon at Holy Angels in Hale Barns, specialising in ecumenism and interfaith relations on behalf of the diocese.

Last November my life hit the buffers through an anonymous historic allegation going back over twenty years. Though I was able to demolish that allegation when at long last after six months the source of the allegation was made known to me, the campaign in the Manchester press has essentially destroyed me. I am now appealing to my past students in the hope that they might be prepared to give a positive account of my years at St Ambrose. [XXXXX XXXXX] suggested that I might approach you in the hope that you might be willing to join the growing list of past students willing to help. Please let me know if you would be willing.

Congratulations on the success of your career, David.

Best wishes,

Alan Morris.

The most telling words in the letter were those relating to a successful career; Professor David Lee is an eminent scientist and climatic expert.

'When I got the email asking me to come forward, defend his teaching and say something good about him, I was completely and utterly gobsmacked,' Lee told me. 'Morris treated boys in three distinct groups: group one was the affluent, the influential, the high-achieving, and he would suck up and curry favour with them, the elite. Category two were similar but were those he was essentially attracted to – the "pretty", good-looking boys. Don't be offended, David, but this is where I would place you! I remember you as a strikingly good-looking, fresh-faced boy. Group three included myself – those whose existence he studiously ignored, actually a form of malice and cruelty in itself.

'I was less than the dust beneath his chariot wheels, as the expression goes: ignored, looked through, non-existent for seven long years. Because of anxieties and insecurities and, indeed, my naïvety, I longed to be acknowledged by this man; to be one of the favoured few – I can't explain why. I feared him and I disliked him but I still wanted his favour. This is probably one of the reasons his memory rather haunts me. So, why all of a sudden would this horrible man remember me? Ah, yes, my "successful career". Yes, a witness titled "Professor" from a university might come in handy, would he not? Apart from anything else, the man was an inveterate snob and sucked up to the rich, the affluent and the influential – he was an Oxbridge graduate and never let anyone forget it.'

Apart from the fact that Morris had ignored him throughout school, there was another reason Lee felt unable to stand up in court for his ex-teacher – because of the things he'd seen Morris do.

'We were in the laboratory and he used to stand at the front with his legs apart and he'd put a kid's head between his legs, with the kid's neck hard up against his groin,' Lee recalled. 'Then he'd take some chalk and he'd make a circular mark on the kid's backside, very slowly and [at the same time as] giving a commentary. I distinctly remember he would get his famous wooden spoon out – then he would slice kids across the bum, not whack them, because that hurt more. I saw him do that three or four times. In later life, I used to semi-jokingly say that I went to school with a bunch of perverts. This was the example I would give. That's why I couldn't possibly defend him and give him a good report. I agonised over whether I should go to the police. I didn't want to open the box of that period of my life. I was a naïve boy and I didn't really understand these things. In later years, I understood the perversity of it.'

Meanwhile, detectives had taken all of their evidence to the Crown Prosecution Service, which would ultimately make the decision as to whether Alan Morris would be charged with any alleged offences. Every statement and all the seized evidence – the DVDs, computers and other items – were reviewed again. By early summer, the CPS had made its decision.

On 15 July 2013 the police returned to Rivington Road to transport Morris to Pendleton for the third time. 'He came into the police station, into the custody office, he stood there and I read through every charge,' said DC Barry Conway. 'He knew he was going to be charged, I'd already told his solicitor, so he had been pre-warned. On that initial point of July 2013 there were forty-seven charges, the majority being indecent assaults. There was one act of outraging public decency and the others were gross indecency with children, which was the scenario of pupils spanking another pupil and him inciting that. It's a procedural thing where we read through every charge, allowing him the opportunity to say anything – which he didn't.'

Morris could not be charged under the more recent Sexual Offences Act; that had come into force in 2004, way after the events at St Ambrose had occurred. Instead, he was charged under the 1956 version of the act, which was in force at the time. This would have an effect on his sentencing if he was found guilty. For example, the 1956 act considered assaults on boys to be worthy of a heftier sentence than those on girls. Other incidents – like the Rivington Road video allegation by Doctor Boy – wouldn't merit a charge under the old law but probably would have done under the newer version. It could still be discussed in court, as evidence of Morris's 'bad character'. So the trial judge would have an eye on both versions of the Sexual Offences Act.

As news of the charges was released, St Ambrose released another statement about the case:

> The police have informed to us that Mr Alan Morris, a former member of staff from some twenty years ago, has been charged with abuse dating back some twenty to thirty years ago. We are deeply shocked by this and are continuing to cooperate fully with the police, as we have throughout the investigation. We note the police have confirmed that no current teachers are involved and parents should have no undue concern. We have contemporary and rigorous child safeguarding polices which we adhere to strictly and take extremely seriously. Our thoughts are with those former pupils and their families but we cannot comment further at this stage.

The statement angered many of the lads. Morris may have left the school's employ in 1995 but he had been at Holy Angels, only yards away, ever since. One successful ex-pupil was particularly incensed. Business Boy contacted me and said that he had a million pounds earmarked to take legal action against the school if, for some reason, Morris got off.

'They put out this daft statement saying Alan Morris had left twenty years ago but he was parading around the school grounds two years ago. Everyone knew what his game was yet he was allowed to go to the church. What's up with that? It's unbelievable. It's bad enough that a few people went through it – but he could have been stopped earlier. You have to do the right thing in life and, if you don't, it comes back and bites you. This stuff has been on my mind for years and years and years. I'm a man of means. If there's something to fight, money won't be an issue. I've got no agenda in this whatsoever – I don't have a dog in the fight. I just want to see justice being done.'

Meanwhile, Alan Morris's next legal port of call was Manchester Magistrate's Court on 26 July, where he would formally respond to the forty-seven charges. Journalists were aware of the court date and were waiting outside to get footage or photographs.

For many ex-pupils, this would have been their first glimpse of Morris for decades. Wearing a dark-blue suit, light-blue shirt and striped tie, he looked much heavier than he did as a teacher. He was walking with a stick and took the steps of the court one at a time, gripping the handrail tightly. I'd completely forgotten about his club foot. Bizarrely, he'd clearly been shopping beforehand, as he was carrying a Marks & Spencer carrier bag.

Such hearings are procedural formalities. Morris only had to confirm his name and where he lived and to deny the charges against him: forty-one of indecent assault, five of gross indecency and one of outraging public decency. He was then given bail and allowed to return to Rivington Road, though there were conditions attached: he wasn't allowed to contact anyone involved in the upcoming trial on the prosecution side, or to have any unsupervised contact with anyone under the age of eighteen.

The cases against Morris were serious enough to be tried in a crown court. As with any matters of this gravity, they entailed a series of hearings and the laying out of a trial timetable. But, in a highly unusual move, it was decided by Judge Timothy Mort to split the evidence across three separate trials. He would oversee all three, the defence and prosecution teams would stay constant but there would be three different juries.

The most serious offences would be top-loaded into trial one. This had pros and cons as far as the detectives were concerned. One of the key strengths of the case against Morris was the sheer number of lads involved – would all of them really have made up similar stories about their ex-teacher and colluded to bring him down? On the other hand, there was so much evidence that it could be too much for one jury to take in. If juries get confused, they can acquit.

The first trial was scheduled to start in June 2014; the second and third trial dates were to be confirmed. But there was a small chance that, if Morris was found guilty at trial one, there might be no need to run trials two and three. If he changed his plea on the run-up to trial one, that could be cancelled too. But this was unlikely, felt those in the know.

'I knew all along he'd plead not guilty for the trial,' says DC Conway. 'He was never, ever going to change his standpoint;

it was always going to lead to a trial. He would never accept responsibility for anything.'

Senior Crown Advocate Charlotte Crangle had been brought on board the case as chief prosecutor. Straight away, she was struck by the unusual nature of those giving evidence.

'In general terms, the victims and witnesses were all well-educated (by virtue of the school they had gone to), respectable, middle-aged men, which is very unusual,' she told me. 'I deal with a lot of sex cases and to have male complainants is rare – so is having such a large number of people who'd done well in their lives in respectable jobs. Because everyone was video-interviewed, that gave me an idea of what kind of witnesses they were going to be, rather than having a paper statement. In the main, they were eloquent men who were struggling to talk about something very personal and intimate.

'I think that, because they *were* men, they were struggling that bit more because they ought to be maintaining a brave face. [But] it struck me that they could properly put into words how they felt because they were all eloquent and intelligent people, even the ones whose lives hadn't gone as well as the others. If you're defending, the first thing you look at is: *where can I chip away at the witnesses' credibility?* If you've got witnesses like this, you know they're going to come across well in court. It adds to the strength of the case.'

As well as the victim interviews, Crangle also went through the police transcripts of Morris's interviews. 'You could really get a flavour of the man from the transcripts – the arrogance came across just on black and white 2D paper. You could tell the way he was responding to the questions

Above left: On my first day of school at St Ambrose in 1972. © *Margaret Nolan*

Above right: Holy Angels Church – next door to St Ambrose College – where Alan Morris became Deacon. © *Katherine Macfarlane*

Below: Me in the 1979 St Ambrose school photo.

Above: The chemistry lab at St Ambrose College – the 'Dark Room' used by Alan Morris to abuse boys is behind the blackboard. © *Greater Manchester Police/SAOB*

Below: The new look St Ambrose in 2014. © *Katherine Macfarlane*

Deacon Alan Morris in the nineties. © Greater Manchester Police

Above: Altrincham Police station, the nerve centre of the Alan Morris case – the biggest historical-abuse investigation ever mounted by Greater Manchester Police.

Below left: DC Barry Conway in one of the video evidence suites where victim testimony was taken.

Below right: DC Nicola Graham outside the Family Support Unit at Altrincham.

All photos © Katherine Macfarlane

Above left: DI Jed Pidd: 'I think that, to some extent, Alan Morris saw the sexual and physical abuse he gave these children as some sort of payment for the education they were receiving at St Ambrose.'

Above right: Charlotte Crangle, the CPS Senior Advocate who prosecuted Alan Morris.

Below: Minshull Street Crown Court, Manchester.   *All photos © Katherine Macfarlane*

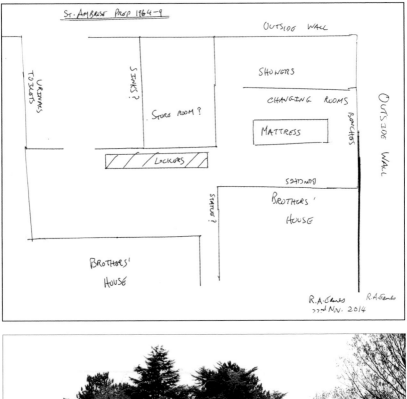

Above: The map of St Ambrose Prep drawn by ex-pupil Richard Eames. Note the mattress marked in the changing rooms.

Below: Woodeaves, the Christian Brothers' house and the one part of the old school that still remains today.   © *Katherine Macfarlane*

WITNESS STATEMENT

CJ Act 1967, s.9; MC Act 1980, ss.5A(3)(a) and 5B; Criminal Procedure Rules 2005, Rule 27.1

URN	06	CU	01	2013

Statement of: **David John Nolan**

Age if under 18: Over 18   (if over 18 insert 'over 18')   Occupation:

This statement (consisting of 4 pages each signed by me) is true to the best of my knowledge and belief and I make it knowing that, if it is tendered in evidence, I shall be liable to prosecution if I have wilfully stated anything in it, which I know to be false, or do not believe to be true.

Signature: X ....   Date: 20 Sept 2013

Check box if witness evidence is visually recorded ☐ *(supply witness details on last page)*

I am David Nolan, I am a former pupil at St Ambrose College, Hale Barns.

In December 2012 I attended Hazel Grove Police station and provided a recorded interview in which I discussed issues at St Ambrose and a chemistry teacher called Mr Morris, I now provide the following statement regarding this matter.

I contacted the police in first place because I had seen the article in the Manchester Evening News which caught my eye straight away because this was the school I went to. The phrase that caught my eye straight away was "extra lessons." There were no names for the teacher in the article but I knew straight away which teacher that referred to and the police request was that if there was anybody at the school at the time could they come forward with information, so that's why I made the initial contact to the police.

The teacher who I immediately thought about re the extra lessons was Alan Morris the chemistry teacher. The three things I wanted to tell the police about were the regime at the school at the time - I think it was very unusual - Alan Morris himself and an incident at the school in around 1979 / 1980 were Alan Morris threatened a whole class of students because he thought somebody had talked about him.

First thing was the regime at St Ambrose. I was there from 1972 to 1981, I spent four years at the prep school and then five years in the senior school. I got a grant to go to the school from the local junior school.

The regime was that corporal punishment was straight through the school, it was everything to the school. Every teacher had their own method and preferred instrument and it was a weekly, daily and sometime hourly occurrence that punishment would be given out. For example during one double music lesson me and another pupil decided to see how many times we could get slippered in a lesson. I got hit 23 times but my friend managed 28 times.

Signature: X ....   Signature witnessed by: ....

'I am David Nolan, I am a former pupil of St Ambrose, Hale Barns.' The first page of the statement I gave to officers investigating Alan Morris.

Above: Alan Morris heading for Minshull Street Crown Court to give his evidence.

Below: 'Will you be remembering the school motto, Mr Morris?' Confronting my old teacher outside court.

All photos © Title Role Productions

that police were asking him, you could feel the patronising way he was dealing with the officers.'

Everyone now had to face an almost year-long wait, until the summer of 2014, for the first trial to begin. DCs Barry Conway and Nicola Graham had the task of making sure all the lads involved stayed on side and didn't change their minds about giving evidence.

'Leading up to the court case, each and every one of them was quite anxious about what to expect,' explained DC Nicola Graham. 'If you've never given evidence, you've no idea, have you? I've been in the police twenty-eight years and I still don't like giving evidence. Most of them said that it wasn't as bad as they'd expected. It's the fear factor. It had been a long time waiting for each and every one of them.'

Officers also had to try to keep the victims apart and told them not to get in touch with other ex-pupils – a strong temptation in the age of social media.

'It was quite a task because we didn't want anyone to say that the victims had colluded with each other,' says DC Graham. 'So we had to make sure we kept them separate – I don't think the victims knew who the other victims were. Before they went to court, Barry and I kept every victim up to date with the progress of the case as best we could over the twenty months of the investigation. Just before the trial, they were all offered a court visit, so they could see exactly what it'd be like. It was a massive task – it's the biggest trial I've ever been involved in.'

In fact, only one ex-pupil changed his mind and withdrew his evidence: me.

My main concern at this stage was that, when the case did come to trial and Morris was, as I genuinely believed he would be, found guilty, 'compassion fatigue' relating to historical-abuse cases would limit the amount of coverage the trial got. I wanted to be there every step of the way to make sure that didn't happen. But the one thing restricting my coverage of the trial was the fact that I was due to give evidence in trial two. Because I was classed as a 'victim', I wasn't allowed to attend trial one at all – and I'd only be allowed to cover trial two after I'd given evidence.

I'd managed to convince the police to let me shadow them during the trial but I hadn't had the go-ahead from the Crown Prosecution Service. If the CPS said no, the police would follow suit and withdraw their offer, leaving me in the position of neither being able to give evidence nor to follow the trail from the inside and then to shout my story from the rooftops: the worst of both worlds.

Despite still not having the CPS's approval, I took a gamble and, on Saturday, 29 March 2014, went to Altrincham unit to meet with DC Nicola Graham and withdraw my evidence. The signed statement said I was doing so for 'professional reasons'. As long as the CPS agreed, I'd now be free to follow the trial as I pleased.

I was spending a huge amount of time with Barry, Jed and Nicola by now and was really getting to like them. For their part, they were putting up with the annoyance of having me around with as much good humour as they could generate. But it had taken meeting after meeting before I managed to gain their trust. The three officers would, I was sure, be vital in convincing other agencies, especially the CPS, that I was one of the good guys and should be allowed inside the investigation.

Not long after I'd withdrawn my evidence, DI Pidd told me that the CPS, fearful that my presence might jeopardise the trial, had said they didn't want me involved in the case anymore.

I vividly recall the frustration building up inside me at the unfairness of it. It felt like the powers that be were trying to silence me – to silence the lads – all over again. It was just like the old days.

I was fizzing with anger and, much to my embarrassment, burst into tears in DI Pidd's office.

Jed and Nicola said they'd do their best to get the CPS to change their mind. In the meantime, I was offered a hug from DC Nicola Graham to keep me going. I said thanks but no thanks.

I'd save that hug until the end of the trial.

CHAPTER EIGHT

T20130755

At 8pm on 23 June 2014 I arrived at the Family Support Unit at a nondescript house to the rear of Altrincham Police Station. It was the first day of Alan Morris's trial. The detectives had, by now, convinced the CPS to allow me to follow the trial's inner workings. I found out later that the thrust of their argument was that I'd be 'easier to manage' if I was inside, rather than outside the investigation. If I was with them, at least they could keep an eye on me.

I'd arranged to meet DC Nicola Graham, to talk to her about how she felt now the moment of truth had arrived. But there were practicalities to deal with first: her car needed loading up with all the case files – hefty blue plastic boxes rammed with all the paperwork generated so far.

The double-stacked boxes filled the back of the family-sized car with the rear seats flattened. We'd talked many times previously about people putting past events 'in a box'. Now those not-so-metaphorical boxes were right there in front of me, full of stories from the past. And they were heavy.

Nicola now had everything she needed for court: the boxes of evidence, plus a change of clothes and a packed lunch for herself and Barry Conway. I asked how she was feeling.

'How are *you* feeling?' she said in return. It was very Nicola that, to turn the tables when I was supposed to be interviewing her.

I told her part of me was aching to go to court and couldn't wait to see Alan Morris... but also that another part of me wished I'd never met her.

I meant that in the nicest possible way. At that point, I felt that I'd much rather the whole thing had never been reopened and had been left hidden away, instead, in one of those boxes. All perfectly normal reactions, she assured me.

Then it was time to go. I'd have to travel separately because there wasn't room in the car for me, what with all the evidence.

'See you in court then,' I said.

(No, I really did. I've always wanted to say that.)

Minshull Street Crown Court is tucked in between Manchester's Piccadilly train station and the city's gay village. It's probably the lesser known of Manchester's two crown courts – the other is a blandly nondescript building across town in an area now known as Spinningfields – but it's the more interesting. It's a striking Grade II listed building that dates back to the late nineteenth century and its overbearing gothic frontage lends it an imposing aura.

Despite this, courts are great levellers – you'll spot criminals having a smoke outside, chatting with barristers, and orange-tinged gangster WAGS sitting side by side with social workers on the landings outside the courtrooms. You'll often see (and, indeed, smell) lads outside the court reeking of drink and weed. It's a fair bet they've been out on bail and are returning to court knowing they're about to get some prison time, so they've been up all night getting wrecked. It'll be the last time in a while.

It had been a long time since I'd covered a trial – not since the late 1990s, probably – and I was feeling a little rusty. So I met up with Ashley Derricott from Granada TV, outside Minshull Street. He's a typical regional-telly news reporter, unsentimental to say the least, but someone I'd known and liked for years.

Journalists like to do the whole rufty-tufty 'I'm dead hard, me' thing and I'm no different, so we did a bit of that. Then Ashley asked how I was feeling about the morning's proceedings... and, to my embarrassment, I burst into tears. Again.

Not a great start. There wasn't a flicker of sympathy from Derricott either.

We headed up the stairs. Going into crown court is a bit like boarding a plane, with a lot of the same procedures and rules. First, you have to have your bags searched – there are obvious no-nos, like knives, but there are other, more subtle rules: you can bring in bottled water but the seal must be unbroken (to stop people bringing in chemicals or flammable liquids), aluminium cans aren't allowed (they could be torn apart and made into a knife) and DVDs/CDs are frowned upon for the same reason.

You go through a metal detector and get the up-and-down treatment from a man with a handheld device before claiming your bag back. A court is essentially a public building – anyone can come in and watch any trial – and so the security measures are there to maintain that sense of openness.

But you're not allowed to audio/visually record any proceedings. In my day, any kind of recording device was likely to be confiscated but, in these days of iPads, smartphones and more, *everything* is a recording device. So now you're allowed to bring them in but reminded not to use them for recording purposes.

(One piece of advice: there are cafes in courts but – trust me – you will want to bring some food with you.)

Once you're in, the next job is to find your court. The video screens said that the case of Regina versus Alan Richard Morris, number T20130755, was to be heard in court nine upstairs.

As Ashley and I headed up the stairs, the first person I saw was Morris, walking unsteadily across the first-floor landing. He'd been as slim as a piece of liquorice back at school; now he was heavily built and leaning on a walking stick.

I'd expected my first sighting of him to be a 'bigger', more dramatic moment. But I felt a bit sorry for him; then I was angry at myself for feeling any sympathy.

Court nine isn't one of those grand, wood-panelled affairs that we're used to seeing in TV dramas – it's more like a local-council meeting room. As you walk in, there's an area to your left for the defendant that's closed in with protective glass. It wasn't that Morris was any kind of danger to the witnesses; it's just that the security measures come with the court.

In front of the defendant are two rows of desks for the defence and prosecution teams, facing the judge, who sits up above them and enters the court via his own doorway. To your right is the public gallery – all are welcome on a first-come-first-served basis – and next to that, the press gallery.

(That's for us journalists, so shift yourselves over.)

Ashley and I took our seats alongside journalists from the *Manchester Evening News* and the *Sale and Altrincham Messenger*. Straight away, we were approached by a clerk, who handed us a piece of paper. It was a Section 39 order. Judge Timothy Mort had decided nothing could be reported about the trial *at all*, for fear of prejudicing the second- and third-trial juries.

In any trial involving crimes of a sexual nature, the identity of the victim, or victims, is not allowed to be reported, nor is anything that could lead to putting several pieces of information together to make a 'jigsaw' ID. That stands in perpetuity – as long as the victim lives, they can never be identified.

Trial one was to be a total media lockdown – no reporting at all until the judge directed otherwise. It wasn't long before all the other journalists had packed up and left, leaving me on my own. There was no way their editors were going to leave them to sit in a court where they weren't going to be able to file any stories for weeks, or even months.

When Morris arrived in court nine – he'd always take the lift because of his disability – he was carrying a briefcase that looked remarkably similar to the one he carried at St Ambrose; the one which used to hold his 'implements'. He took his seat

143

behind the glass, put on a set of headphones to help him hear what was going on and pulled out a clipboard. He popped his pen and immediately began taking notes.

No matter what was being said over the next four weeks, he never looked up. Sometimes, if the testimony was particularly emotional or was being addressed directly to him, he closed his eyes and rested his chin on his walking stick, seemingly zoning out from the proceedings. He never gave any indication that there was anyone else there in the courtroom.

'He never changed his expression,' noted DC Conway. 'He was quite static, very emotionless. He never changed the way he was – very poker-faced, barely a flicker throughout.'

After the usual legal arguments – housekeeping and procedural points that the jury doesn't see but that the journalists are allowed to watch – the jury came in. There were six men and six women, a genuine mixture: some seemed very young – one girl appeared to be barely twenty – and the eldest was a man in his sixties.

As things got underway, the contrasting styles of the two barristers soon became apparent. Had he been an actor, Hugh McKee, for the defence, was exactly the person you would cast as a barrister. Round and red of face, boomy of voice and with an apparent default setting of 'a bit cross', the folks in the public gallery soon nicknamed him Rumpole.

For the prosecution, Charlotte Crangle seemed equally well cast. Blonde, tall and quietly spoken, she would play an almost sisterly role to the procession of damaged lads who passed through the court to give evidence.

Crangle – a senior advocate for the CPS – had reviewed

all the lads' evidence and the transcripts of Morris's police interviews. Based on the number of people who came forward and the similarity of their accounts, her first thought was, 'Why is he not pleading guilty? I only prosecute but, before I started working for the CPS, I defended as well. I looked at the evidence and thought, *I'm so glad I'm prosecuting this, rather than having to defend him.*'

Judge Mort slightly bucked any expectation you might have had. He was achingly well-spoken and a little imperious, which comes with the territory. (When the judge walks into the court, you stand up; when the judge walks out, you stand up again, just like we used to do at school.) But he was also kindly and gentle and spoke to everyone, Morris included, in a caring and decent manner. I liked him straight away.

I scanned the public gallery to see if there was anyone I recognised. I'd come prepared – in my bag, I'd brought copies of a letter I was planning to give to anyone who looked familiar. The CPS had ordered that I wasn't allowed to speak to any ex-pupils until after they'd spoken in court. So I was planning to approach witnesses, introduce myself and give them the letter afterwards. It read,

Hi – my name is David Nolan and I was at St Ambrose from '72 to '81 – Alan Morris was my teacher.

I can't praise you enough for coming forward and giving evidence.

I was due to give evidence in the case myself, but I've withdrawn it on the advice of the police and the CPS to work on a book about the school and the Morris story. The aim is to get more people to come forward and tell police about events from the past. The police are fully supporting this – Nicola and Barry from Greater Manchester Police have been incredibly helpful.

Please could you help me? Please can you get in touch – just for a talk?

David Nolan

The trial proper got underway with Charlotte Crangle's opening statement for the prosecution:

'This case involves what the prosecution say is a sustained campaign of abuse against large numbers of schoolboys under the care of the defendant in his role as a teacher and, therefore, protector of their interests. The abuse took place between the early 1970s and 1990 and was characterised by the defendant physically chastising various pupils at the school and using that contact with them to further his own sexual desires. The prosecution say that the chastisement was, perhaps, in some cases deserved but [that] it was conducted in an inappropriate manner and used as a cloak for a more sinister motive, namely the deriving of sexual pleasure through such contact with the boys.'

Then there were the victims and witnesses – the 'boys' that Charlotte had spoken of. Now, of course, they were men of my age, some a little older or younger, but all with stories and experiences to tell of. Some were angry, some were nervous, some were downright scared but their stories, when laid out one after the other, had a chillingly similar ring to them.

There's something deeply troubling about watching a

146

middle-aged man shaking with nerves as he recounts events from decades earlier that still weigh heavily upon him. I hated watching it. I wanted to interrupt Hugh McKee's defence cross-examinations and shout out, 'Leave him alone, I know he's telling the truth!'

One ex-pupil – a burly man in his fifties – gave the impression he could handle most things in life. He was broad-shouldered and thick-necked but looked like he'd rather be anywhere else than in court nine.

'I'm a big man now,' he told the jurors, 'but I was a small boy then.'

He told the jury about Alan Morris beating him with a rubber hose then, on the next occasion, offering to use his open hand. He told how his backside had been smacked as he lay across the teacher's lap; Morris then indecently assaulted him, touching him as he pushed his erection against the schoolboy. It happened again a few weeks later.

The witness talked about the culture of beatings and bullying at the school – how he could handle them but he couldn't cope with what had happened in the Dark Room. The few minutes in that room with 'him over there', as he referred to Alan Morris, had altered his life forever, affecting his sexual development and robbing himself of his Catholic faith. He'd kept it inside himself all these years.

'After thirty-nine years, I've said my piece,' he said, before leaving the stand to a pin-drop silence. The jury seemed almost relieved when his testimony was over.

'The man who told us it had affected his sex life,' recalls prosecutor Charlotte Crangle, 'a grown man in the witness

147

box in tears telling the jury that, even though it was two short-lived incidents, it has constantly affected his ability to have a normal sexual relationship with his wife and led to divorce in his first marriage – that was very powerful evidence.'

Reminding the jury that these hefty blokes in their forties and fifties were once just skinny slips of lads was a key part of the prosecution's job.

'We asked everyone if they had photographs of themselves at school or school reports,' says Crangle, 'to give the jury a flavour of what they were like as boys. But a big bloke on the verge of tears giving his evidence, telling the court the impact this has had on his life and relationships, is still very powerful. For many of them, it's the giving of the evidence that's the therapeutic bit, not what happens to Alan Morris in the end. It's being brave enough to come forward first of all, then to come to court and give evidence in front of a room full of strangers. It's helped quite a few of them.'

When he cross-examined the ex-pupils, McKee for the defence seemed to be trying to plant seeds of doubt in the jury's minds about dates and details – he would read out lists of other ex-pupils' names and stop when the witness said they didn't remember that particular contemporary. It was as if to say, *this guy's memory isn't so hot; perhaps his recollections about the other stuff are unsound too?*

'I can't remember the date but I remember he had brown trousers on,' one victim countered, getting frustrated with the line of questioning.

Charlotte Crangle soon coined a catchphrase: 'It's OK, it's not a memory test.' She said it to many of the ex-pupils giving evidence but it was clearly aimed at the jury. Like the defence, she was trying to relay an almost subliminal message: *it doesn't matter if this was May or April of 1976; listen to what the guy is saying and hear the hurt in his voice.*

Everything possible is done at court to prevent the witnesses or victims encountering the accused. Not only because it could be highly upsetting for them but also because they could change their mind about giving evidence. They come into court through a separate door and wait in a 'witness suite'. Volunteers are always on hand to escort them whenever they're in the building. They make sure that the accused is already sat down in the court before the witnesses are sent for, so there's no chance of bumping into the person who may have victimised them. But accidents do happen.

'A few people accidentally saw him [Morris] outside the court during that first trial,' confirms Barry Conway. 'They inadvertently spotted him as they were coming into court. They were shaking because they'd actually seen him. It must have been that fear and that apprehension of what was going to come, knowing you haven't been able to do anything about it since you were a twelve, thirteen, fourteen-year-old child.'

During the Morris trial, there was an additional headache – the need to keep all of the ex-pupils apart. Most of the victims didn't know who the other victims were and detectives were concerned they'd be accused of allowing collusion between the lads. Many were given individual rooms in the witness suites, remaining oblivious as to the identities of their counterparts.

Doctor Boy took the stand and told how he'd visited Rivington Road on the pretext of 'extra lessons', only to be confronted by a porn video and a masturbating Alan Morris. He also told them about his other run-ins with Morris and what he'd seen the teacher do to younger pupils. Though it was his evidence that had opened the floodgates this time around – indeed, he was the reason we were all in court nine – he took no pleasure in being there.

'I was very anxious about going to court,' Doctor Boy told me later. 'You didn't know how many people were involved – it might be just your evidence against his evidence. What did I have? I had something from twenty-odd years ago that was my word against his. What evidence did I have? Almost nothing. I didn't know what other evidence there was, so I felt very vulnerable about it and that it could go absolutely nowhere.'

Doctor Boy's father accompanied him on the day he gave evidence and became a familiar face in the public gallery, studiously taking notes (which he was reprimanded for) and sending out waves of bonhomie to the mismatched band of parents, old boys, friends of friends, law students, police officers, social workers and rubberneckers in the public gallery. Everyone liked Doctor Dad – he had a way of keeping everyone's sprits up. But his attitude towards the trial and his son's involvement was unexpected, to say the least.

'I believed it was a mistake for the police to have ever brought the case against Morris,' he told me. 'That was my view at the time. I remember saying to one of the officers, "I think this is a waste of public money. I think there's an element of homophobia and I think the police have been dragged into this because, when they first interviewed Morris, he would have been extremely pompous and talked down to them and they've got hooked on, "We're going to get this guy." That was my initial feeling.'

'My dad's a very analytical character,' explains Doctor Boy. 'He likes one plus one is two. But court is about weight of evidence and the opinion of the jury. That's how it's worked for hundreds of years. It's not binary. When we talk about evidence, we want photographs. We want hardcore proof. When it's historical, it could be flaky, very subjective, not very convincing. My dad described the evidence as being like looking at an impressionistic painting: close up, it's just dots. But when you stand back, you can see the whole picture. At the start, he didn't get the dots.'

Initially, Doctor Dad just came for the day; then he decided to stay almost throughout the whole process: 'I went to the trial to support my son. He'd been in quite a difficult place for a long time. We knew he was in quite an emotional state, he was not looking forward to going, so, as a father-son thing, I said I'd go, just to be there to talk with him so that afterwards – he couldn't remember what he'd said in court – I could offer some sort of judgement of whether he'd got it right and was a credible witness. So I went along for that, then I got absorbed quite quickly. I became hooked. I'd never been to a trial before. I was intrigued by the style. We see the confrontations on TV: "Objection!" "Objection overruled!" There's none of that.'

Meanwhile, I was working my way through the people in the gallery, introducing myself, striking up conversations, gently asking them why they were there and handing out copies of my letter. Some were unsurprisingly wary; others began to talk.

'One of my friends was involved in the first trial – I took

him to court on the morning of his evidence,' one 'Gallery Boy' who used to attend St Ambrose told me. 'Another couple of lads I hadn't seen for thirty years were involved as well. I wanted to see who was there. Did I recognise anyone? I recognised a few people.'

What was clear was that ex-pupils still held onto a simmering anger about their time at St Ambrose, decades later. It was feelings like these that seemed to have drawn them to court nine, as much as the presence of Alan Morris.

'On a good day I didn't like the school – on a bad day I hated it,' Gallery Boy told me. 'Over-the-top control and disproportionate corporal punishment, that was what it was about. It was five years of abnormality. I loved my primary school. I loved the college I went to afterwards. But Ambrose? There were some very strange things going on.'

As ex-pupils like Gallery Boy looked on, the testimonies continued. Victims and witnesses told the court how they'd been taken to the Dark Room by Morris. One pupil claimed that, aged about thirteen, Morris had taken him out of school and driven him to a cemetery some miles away. While they were there, Morris took out his penis and started masturbating. The ex-pupil told his sister about the incident when he was in his twenties – she later came forward on his behalf when Morris was arrested in 2012.

The jury heard about the various devices that Morris used, including the Paddywhack – a flesh-coloured leather paddle similar to a table-tennis bat. They heard how he thrived on power and control. It was even claimed that Morris's attacks on pupils went on after they'd left the school.

One pupil told that, after leaving, he'd been asked to come back to St Ambrose to return some books. Perhaps as an indicator of the power Morris wielded over the boys, the teenager agreed but couldn't find all of the books he'd borrowed.

'He was told to go into the stockroom and told to bend over,' Charlotte Crangle told the jury. 'The defendant could not find the slipper that he was going to use and so used a metre-long board ruler. After the first blow to his buttocks, [the witness] jumped up but the defendant placed his hand onto the teenager's bottom and said he didn't think that he had been punished enough. He continued the punishment but, this time, using his hand, seeming to prolong the contact between hand and bottom unnecessarily. He then told the ex-pupil that his bottom was still not hot enough and [that] he would have to pull his pants down, proceeding to undo his button and zip while pressing his groin up against the teenager. The defendant then pulled the boy's trousers and underpants down and they fell to the floor, whereby he was hit twice more – once to each buttock cheek. The defendant went on to pull his own pants down, saying this was to make the teenager feel better, and, again, pressed himself up against him while delivering two more blows. At this point, he could feel the defendant's erect penis rubbing next to his bottom and the defendant reached around and touched the boy's penis and testicles. After fifteen seconds or so, the defendant then pulled the teenager's trousers back up, after which he was allowed to leave.'

Again, the defence had their opportunity to cross-examine the witness, who batted away Hugh McKee's questions.

'The way in which he responded to the questions from the defence was very powerful,' Charlotte Crangle later told me. 'It was almost as though [he was saying], *of course this is the truth; why are you asking me these stupid questions?*'

From the public gallery, relatives, ex-pupils and the merely curious looked on as life at St Ambrose – the life I'd known only too well – was laid out before the jury.

'I was sitting with some lads who'd been to Ambrose,' recalls Doctor Dad. 'One had been in my son's class. We were listening to evidence about Morris getting an erection – really graphic. One of them leaned over and said, "This is surreal!"'

Ex-pupil Andy Rothwell, now a successful sports agent, came to give evidence as a witness, telling the jury about the time he was told to cane his classmates on camera.

'I was glad to see [Morris] in court,' Rothwell told me. 'I wasn't looking for retribution, I was looking for justice. I was surprised how he was in court: he never looked at me, or the jury or the barristers or the judge; he kept his head down. It looked like he was writing notes. You read about things in the papers but you don't ever think you'll be in court with your view being taken seriously. It's only recently, when you saw these cases coming forward, that you started to question yourself: *Was it right?* Obviously, it wasn't right – what's right about being asked to hit your friends and him taking photos?'

Another ex-pupil told how he'd seen Morris bounce a boy upside down so his head was against his lap. He'd been deeply disturbed by it. Later, Morris had told the boy to come to the Dark Room at lunchtime. He'd been too freaked out to go but, when Morris caught up with him, he grabbed the pupil by the throat, pushed him up against a wall and threw him down several flights of steps.

'He was out of control,' the former pupil told the jury. This witness was asked if his current profession somehow coloured his view of how Morris had behaved. I made a point of looking at the jury's faces when the witness told them he was now the headmaster of a prestigious private school.

As well as testimonies concerning Morris, witness after witness also told stories about the school itself and the culture of corporal punishment woven into the very fabric of St Ambrose. Beatings were 'random' and 'endemic', the regime was 'violent and abusive'.

'We just shouldered it and carried on,' one ex-pupil said.

Paul Wills had travelled from his remote home in Scotland to give evidence. For Wills, like many of the lads, the world of police detectives, barristers and judges was a new one: 'I was nervous. I've never been to court before. They got me in the day before and gave me a look around the court and told me what would happen. But, when I walked in the dock, I forgot all that. I was just up for a fight. I felt aggressive towards the [defence] barrister. I had no idea what the barrister was going to do but I knew there'd be cross-examination. I didn't have any issues with it because I wasn't lying. If I was a defendant and I was lying, I could see it being really hard but all I had to do was tell them exactly what happened. It wasn't rehearsed – if you've never been to court, you can't rehearse it. Why did I agree to testify? It's not even personal anymore. It's like bacteria: you're trying to get rid of it as a matter of public or social health.'

CHAPTER NINE

A LEGITIMATELY
SCARY GUY

As the trial progressed, I noticed a barrister in wig and gown who didn't appear to be engaging directly in proceedings. He was certainly taking a full interest but he wasn't actually doing anything. I did a little digging and discovered he wasn't there to represent either Alan Morris or the lads; he was there on behalf of the insurers. If Morris was found guilty, those lads who'd been seeking compensation would be in for a payout. The trial wasn't just about getting justice for the victims or punishing the guilty, it was also about money.

Looking at the faces of the jurors as the trial continued, I tried to gauge how they were taking all the information. Several were young – in their early to mid-twenties. Descriptions of Christian Brothers in flowing black costumes, dishing out strappings and canings, must have seemed like stories of a distant planet to them. Were they religious? Would they find the idea of Deacon Alan Morris – a man who'd dedicated himself to God and taken a vow of celibacy – sitting at home with a stash of punishment porn too much to believe? I found it hard to take on board some of the stuff I was hearing and I'd seen a lot of it at first hand.

At the heart of this was the testimony of the lads themselves. From where I was sitting, their evidence was breaking through the barrier created by all the time that had elapsed. It gave the jury a fairly stark choice between two separate versions of events: either all of these men who came from different generations of the school had colluded to concoct a series of experiences that were remarkably similar... or they were, quite simply, all telling the truth.

Quietly, the detectives were delighted with the way things were going. But there would be one evidential hiccup that would end in a moment of high drama.

One ex-pupil had told police how Morris had taken him to a graveyard and masturbated in front of him. He also described being in the Dark Room and getting hit with the Paddywhack.

'He said [he] could feel the defendant standing next to him while he was doing this,' Charlotte Crangle told the jury, 'like he was rubbing himself up against him.' But, when the witness appeared in court, his evidence didn't go quite as far as his police statement.

'He was very nervous about giving his evidence,' confirms DC Barry Conway. 'He was vulnerable and he had personal issues. The long-term effects on him were massive. He was always willing to turn up and give evidence but it was a really big thing and it took a lot out of him. The incident in the school didn't quite come up to the standard of proof. The incident in the graveyard was originally outraging public decency – there was a point of law: someone else had to be able to view what was going on. The judge ruled them both to be "not guilty" verdicts but they were both still used as evidence of bad character, to show Morris's sexual interest in boys.'

Having plucked up the courage to tell his story, the ex-pupil was bitterly disappointed about the way things had gone in court nine. 'He was upset that the indictments related to him had been "not guiltys",' DC Conway told me. 'He felt he'd let himself down, let us down, let his mum and dad down. He hadn't, of course, but there were all kinds of emotions going on.'

The witness left court but those emotions would come back in dramatic fashion before the trial ended. Meanwhile, Mike Bishop – the lad whose tie Alan Morris liked to twirl, who had an X 'marking the spot' on his backside in chalk – took the stand and personified the challenge that the prosecution faced.

Bishop is now in his early forties and cuts a burly figure. The jury needed to be reminded that he was twelve or thirteen when these incidents took place; a mere slip of a lad. Like many of the victims, he now had a good job and was used to talking in public. That all seemed to leave him as he took the stand.

'Coming into court and knowing I was going to see the man I've been most scared of for my entire existence was petrifying, absolutely petrifying,' he told me. 'I walked in and I purposely didn't look to my left. I was told where he was going to be as I'd already done a tour of the court. But, unfortunately, curiosity got the better of me and I looked. It was at that point that I couldn't get my oath out.

'Then I thought, *I'm not going to be scared anymore*. And I looked at him: *I'm not scared of you. I'm here to bury you.* It sounds really angry now – [but] I'm not angry anymore. At the time I thought, *I'm here to tell everybody what you did and you shouldn't be getting away with this.*

'When I looked at him, I had nothing but pity for him, genuinely. All my nervousness, all my tension, all my stress seemed to leave me.'

Bishop opted to have the video evidence he gave to the Altrincham team played in court, rather than going through all the details again. He was then to be questioned by both the prosecution and the defence.

'I don't think I could have stood there and recounted what had happened in front of him' he said. 'Not because it wasn't true but because you almost expected him to stand up and start smashing stuff, like he did at school! Coming in and walking past the public galleries was all right. I think you [David Nolan] were ahead of me as I came in. The jury scared the crap out of me. Then I saw one guy get up and he was wearing shorts and it was kind of bizarre because you expect juries to be in suits and ties and all that stuff, especially in a case like this.'

The court heard how Morris would take Bishop to an empty classroom while 'on patrol' at the school and find an excuse to spank him, putting a chalk target on his backside. The teacher was, Bishop told the jury, 'a legitimately scary guy.'

Bishop was also quizzed over the details of his evidence – he was pushed on specific dates and, like many of the ex-pupils, asked to say who he remembered from a list of names. Hugh McKee, for the defence, even queried Bishop's use of the word 'suit' to describe Alan Morris's attire.

'He wore this brown suit at school,' Bishop remembered. 'The barrister said, "I put it to you that he hardly ever wore a suit except on special occasions – I put it to you that he wore a jacket and trousers." And my response was, "To a twelve-year-old boy, that constitutes a suit." The judge jumped in then and said to the jury, "Just for the avoidance of doubt, what he was wearing in this case can be classed as a suit."

'I thought, *Even you* [Mr McKee] *know the game is up. The questions you're asking me about whether or not he wore a suit… whether it was March or April 1988 or 1989… why I can't remember who was in the class with me… you're dead, you've got nothing. I win. I've won. If that's all you're going to ask me, if that's all you're going to talk to me about, you haven't got a leg to stand on here.*

'And I kind of got a little bit arrogant, a little bit smug at that point and I was quick in my remarks back to the barrister – probably not in my favour – but I thought, *I'm not going to stand here being scared anymore.*'

Bishop's mother – the woman who had complained about Morris's behaviour to the school – was with him when he went to court.

'When it was over, there was a huge, huge outpouring,' he told me. 'It was the release; it was the overwhelming feeling that everything now had been done. I couldn't do any more – I said what I'd said, I'd done what I'd done. I was walking down the street between the car park and Minshull Street and I said to my mum, "Just give me a minute," and I walked away and fell apart. They left me alone for about five or six minutes. I came back and I said, "I'm OK, I'm fine now, I'm done."'

Derek Scanlan travelled all the way from the Outer Hebrides to give his account of what happened to him and other lads in the chemistry lab all those years ago. Like many of the ex-pupils, when he walked into court, it wouldn't be the first time he saw the room.

'Strangely, just before the case, Nicola took me up to the courtroom to let me look at it,' Scanlan later told me. 'We walked right into Morris as we walked into the building – he didn't recognise me. It wasn't a very nice experience. He has a kind of evil aura about him.'

Morris studiously ignored most of the lads as they gave evidence – but he couldn't seem to take his eyes off Scanlan. 'The police kept saying, "He won't look at you during the case." But he did look at me. He kept looking because he obviously didn't know who I was. I just kept looking straight back at him. I finally got to say in public what that man had done to young boys. I remember looking at the jury and some of them looked absolutely horrified. The defence barrister was hopeless: he was trying to trick me. The judge stepped in at one point. I was surprised [by] how short the defence questioning was. I think they realised they had little to gain from keeping us in the dock.'

Having said his piece, Derek went downstairs to the witness area. He and his old school friend, Paul Wills, were both congratulated by prosecution barrister Crangle. But Scanlan had mixed feelings about the experience. 'I'd put it behind me... and, suddenly, it's there all over again,' he said.

Scott Morgan – the ex-prep boy who'd damaged his eye at the school – also gave evidence. He told the jury that, at one stage, he spent nearly every lunchtime in the chemistry lab with Morris. But, when he put him under cross-examination, McKee tried to paint a very different picture.

'It was surreal,' Morgan told me. 'He put it to me that Mr Morris was my best friend in the school and that he looked after me. No. He wasn't. I just looked at him and shook my head. They couldn't have been further from the truth.'

For some of the lads, giving evidence was a great release; a moment they'd waited and longed for. Win or lose, they'd had their day in court.

But life is not always as cut and dried as that. Scott would later tell me that, unlike some of the others, he wished that he hadn't given evidence in the trial at all.

'I regret it now,' he says. 'It would have been easier not to go to the trial in the first place. Part of you thinks, *Did I do the right thing?* I tried to bury it all twenty-odd years ago because I wanted nothing to do with the school. This has brought it all back. I went into the court thinking I'd get closure, and you don't. What he did degenerated from the odd smacking to getting your pants down and prodding you with stuff because he could get away with it. That's what hurts – not standing up to him at the time and saying something about it. It was accepted. He didn't pay any attention whatsoever when I gave evidence. It was like he didn't care. It was like he'd shut himself into another world. I got the impression from the trial that he didn't recognise that he'd done anything wrong. And he never will.'

Of all the witnesses and victims who went through court nine that first week, there was one lad whose testimony I was waiting for. The Altrincham detectives didn't know it but I'd found out that one of the victims was someone I was really friendly with at school, who I'd lost contact with. I hoped that, if I could catch his eye when he gave evidence, he might recognise me and agree to talk.

When his testimony was due, I positioned myself at the top of the steps inside the building, where the victims had to walk up to get to the doors of court nine. I had photos of us together as kids, in case he didn't recognise me – as we hadn't seen each other for thirty years or more.

At the allotted time, my old school friend walked up the stairs. He spotted me and I saw him mouth what appeared to be the words, 'Fucking hell, it's David Nolan!'

He recognises me then.

There was a court volunteer with him and I was mindful of the fact that, at the CPS's insistence, I wasn't allowed to approach any victims until after they'd given evidence. I mouthed the words, 'I'm not allowed to talk to you,' and made a cutting gesture across my throat with my hand. He seemed to understand. I couldn't think of what else to do, so I made a slightly shit 'power to the people' gesture with my fist.

Ground Zero Boy did the same before he entered the court. It turned out that it was my old school friend who'd approached police about Morris in 2001, when they'd decided not to take matters any further. I'd had no idea until he turned up to give his evidence.

Describing himself as a 'lively' kid, Ground Zero told the jury how Morris would smack his bottom with his bare hand, 'rub it better' and push his erection against his backside. He recounted how he'd be beaten with the cane, the strap and a long wooden board ruler, and told of a bizarre incident when Morris offered to put a piece of buttock-shaped carpet down his underpants, apparently to soften the blows of the cane. Ground Zero allowed him to do it, noting how he touched his backside as he did so.

Morris would bend him over a stool in the Dark Room and draw out the beatings – whacking his cane into the walls and furniture to ramp up the fear. 'He would try to freak you out, psych you out,' Ground Zero said. 'It was slow, teasing, he'd string you along. He'd milk it.'

The court also heard how Morris had made Ground Zero stand on a table in front of the other boys, as he held a flame from a Bunsen burner near the boy's crotch. As I heard this testimony, a weird thought came to me: *I was in the classroom when that happened*. But up to that point, I'd completely forgotten about it.

Ground Zero said the beatings, the touching, the rubbing, the encounters in the Dark Room went on, week in, week out, for three years. Again, I'd never realised it.

Of all the lads, Ground Zero spent the longest time on the witness stand and faced the fiercest cross-examination. He described the cat-and-mouse game of confession he'd played with Alan Morris on the telephone in 2001, after the police had decided not to pursue the case. He was accused of carrying out a vendetta after leaving school with minimal qualifications. It was claimed Morris had laughed at him when he picked up the certificates for the two O-levels he'd managed to gain at the age of sixteen.

The jury heard claims that Ground Zero had threatened to ruin Morris, using his apparent expertise with computers to make life a misery for him, blackening his name online and ruining his reputation. They also heard how the idea of putting carpet inside his underpants to protect himself from blows had been Ground Zero's, not Morris's.

A letter was produced, written many years earlier, in which Ground Zero politely asked for help in tracing a film he'd appeared in, shot by drama teacher Sam Wilkinson. The defence wanted to know how it was possible for someone to write such a letter to someone who had abused him. They also pointed out that Ground Zero had attended Wilkinson's funeral when he died in 2007. He'd approached Morris and the two had chatted – surely not the way an abused boy would interact with his abuser.

Ground Zero kept his voice calm and his answers clear. He was far better at it than I would have been. He told the jury he'd drawn a line under the whole thing years earlier and that, if he met Alan Morris outside court, after giving evidence, he'd shake his hand and have a perfectly polite conversation with him.

'I'm not someone who is full of wrath,' Ground Zero told the court. 'I pity him.'

This was an altogether tougher line of questioning than I'd

heard so far. My main concern about giving evidence before I withdrew had been losing my temper on the witness stand. When someone is essentially calling you a liar, it's hard not to get riled.

'I always say to a witness, it will feel like these questions are a personal attack on you but they're not,' says Senior Crown Advocate Charlotte Crangle. 'It's important to keep that at the back of your mind when you're giving evidence. No matter how personal it feels, it isn't. But, if you find yourself getting angry or upset, that's a natural reaction and I wouldn't want to stop a witness feeling that. It's a lot better these days than it used to be – not just the questioning but the way that it's done. Defence counsels have got to do their job and put their case. But judges are much more proactive at stepping in and stopping inappropriate questioning. They're much more conscious of not giving the defence a free reign to do that. A lot of defence counsels also realise now that the more aggressive they are with the witness, the more sympathy a jury may have for that witness, so it often backfires. [Aggressive questioning is] something to be used very sparingly. Often it's used when a witness is hostile. It's not used much these days – it's not like it is on telly.'

When he'd finished his testimony, Judge Timothy Mort thanked Ground Zero, and the former St Ambrose pupil left the witness stand.

I ran out just ahead of him, holding the doors of court nine open as he exited. We grabbed hold of each other and hugged. I burst into tears – again.

'It's all right, mate,' he said, despite that fact that it was him who'd just been through the ordeal of court, not me. The court volunteer who was with him got quite caught up in the moment. I took out the photos of me and Ground Zero from the 1970s to show her.

'You've both kept your looks,' she lied. Later, I heard she'd gone back downstairs to the witness area and told the other court staff about the two blokes hugging and crying outside court nine. She was in tears.

Ground Zero and I went for a cup of tea. We had a lot to catch up on.

'Hand on heart, I didn't feel much,' he said when I asked about seeing Morris in court. 'I'd dealt with it by then. He's irrelevant to me. It's never been quite real, what happened. But it shows that a perverse paedophile can look like the bloke next door. It can be anyone. It doesn't have to be someone you'd cower from. I could stand next to Alan Morris now and I wouldn't bat an eyelid but, with hindsight, I find it hard to believe that anyone can be that twisted and appear to be a normal functioning person. But now I know.'

As the first week of the trial drew to an end and the last of the lads gave their evidence, the officers in the case prepared for the main attraction. How would Morris fare in the dock?

While waiting around for the final session of the week, I spoke to DC Conway about how he felt things were going. Barry was very cautiously optimistic. We talked a little about getting Morris on the stand the following week. He said the whole thing was a bit ironic, given the St Ambrose school motto – that bit of Latin on the badge of our school blazer. I didn't have the heart to say that not only did I not remember it, I'd never bothered to find out what it meant the whole time I was there.

That night I looked it up. It was *Vitam Impendere Vero* and it seemed to have a variety of translations, all with a similar thrust: 'To Devote One's Life to the Truth', 'Life Depends on Truth', or even 'To Lay Down One's Life for Truth'. I'd walked around with that written on my blazer for nine years and it never occurred to me to find out what it meant.

Thanks to DC Conway, now I knew.

CHAPTER TEN

VITAM IMPENDERE VERO

On Monday, 30 June 2014 – the beginning of the second week of the trial – I arrived outside Minshull Street court at 8.30pm. I was waiting for Alan Morris to take the stand for the first time, so it seemed like the ideal moment to reintroduce myself to him. I hadn't seen him for thirty-three years – not since he'd written 'The Battle Is Over' on my final report card. It appeared he'd been wrong. The battle was far from over.

Cameraman Ian Bradshaw was with me, along with researcher Laura Robinson, who was handling the sound – we were going to film the encounter for posterity and maybe see if we could convince someone to broadcast it after the trials were over. I'd been struggling in terms of what I should actually say to Morris. What was the right way to play it? I'd only have one chance. Then I remembered what DC Barry

Conway had said to me about the St Ambrose school motto: *Vitam Impendere Vero...*

I was also concerned about how best to approach Morris on a physical level. I was very much aware that he now walked with a stick and I didn't want to appear to be chasing a disabled man down the street. Instead, I found a position near the court steps, where he'd have to pass between me and the camera, and waited.

And waited. And waited.

One hour and twenty minutes later, he finally appeared, accompanied by a young clerk. The court entrance at Minshull Street is right next to the Metrolink tram line, which, at the time, was overlooked by a building site, so it was very noisy. I was going to have to shout. As Morris drew near, I started to yell at the teacher who'd yelled at me so many times all those years ago:

'Mr Morris, it's David Nolan, one of your ex-pupils! Do you remember me, Mr Morris?' The drills from the building site were kicking in by this stage, so I really had to yell.

'ARE YOU LOOKING FOWARD TO TELLING YOUR SIDE OF THE STORY, MR MORRIS? WILL YOU BE REMEMBERING THE SCHOOL MOTTO, MR MORRIS? IT'S *VITAM IMPENDERE VERO*. IT WAS ON THE BADGE ON OUR SCHOOL BLAZERS. IT MEANS LIFE DEPENDS ON TRUTH... LIFE DEPENDS ON TRUTH!'

Morris, who had probably been briefed to ignore any approaches outside court, steadfastly stared at the ground as he slowly passed by. I'd like to state for the record that, despite the delicacy of the situation, I displayed steely professional determination. I'd like to but I'd be lying. The truth is that my hands were shaking, I was a touch shrill and the whole thing made me feel a bit sick and dizzy.

I took a breather before going in. Another ex-pupil, Neil Summers, had been in touch; he wanted to see the case at first hand, so we met up outside the court. We went through the usual searches and scans and made our way up to court nine. When the barristers arrived, it became very clear that the head of Morris's defence team, Hugh McKee, was not a happy man.

I took my seat in the press gallery with Neil; it's situated just behind the witness stand, so people giving evidence have their backs to the journalists. I could hear grumblings across the court: 'It's not on... I'm not having it,' muttered Mr McKee to prosecutor Charlotte Crangle.

When Judge Timothy Mort entered, we all stood. McKee was straight on the case – he wanted to complain to His Honour about my behaviour. He had contempt of court in mind. He told Judge Mort that Mr Morris was 'distressed and intimidated' by what I'd done and that, at the very least, I should be removed from the press gallery. Although I knew I'd kept calm during the encounter, there was something strangely satisfying about hearing this.

Distressed and intimidated? Now you know how we felt, Mr Morris.

Judge Mort asked me to identify myself and I put up my hand. *I'm back at school again*, I thought.

He looked sternly at me over the top of his glasses. I braced myself for what is known in legalistic terms as a 'bollocking'. Judge Mort did, indeed, bollock me but I could have sworn he did it with a little twinkle in his eye. Perhaps he approved of my use of Latin – I was clearly a better class of heckler.

But he told me what I'd done had been 'ill thought out and badly timed.' My first instinct on hearing this was to say I'd spent a very long time thinking about it and, what was more, the timing was perfect as it was the first day of Morris's testimony. But there are certain times in life when you should keep your trap shut and midway through being bollocked by a crown court judge is probably one of them.

After the dressing-down, Judge Mort told me to move from the press gallery to the public gallery – the *back* of the public gallery, he added for good measure. It really was just like being back at school. But I got a good welcome from ex-pupils and parents when I took my seat. I felt that, after this happened, I was accepted a bit more by the folks in the public gallery.

In a true display of St Ambrosian stubbornness, Neil Summers took the view that, as he hadn't done anything wrong, he'd stay exactly where he was – which he did for the rest of the day.

At 11.26am that same morning, Alan Morris took the stand for the first time. I could actually see him better from the public gallery and it was a fascinating, if rather chilling, experience. His gait was ungainly and he walked over to the stand with the aid of his stick. His once reed-thin physique was now bloated but his face was remarkably unchanged.

When taking the oath and swearing by Almighty God that the evidence he gave would be the truth, he made a point of pausing and over-emphasising the word 'TRUTH' for dramatic effect. In a raw, raspy voice, he recounted the details of his education and career. He talked about his childhood and contracting polio, his schooling, gaining a place at Cambridge and his early days at St Ambrose.

He kept leaning in too close to the microphone and 'popping' as his breath hit the outside of the mic cover. He told how he used to hit boys on the bottom because it was less painful for them and how use of the cane brought 'good order' to the school. He used canes bought from a garden centre; he hated the strap but did tell of how he'd strapped one boy for letting off a stink bomb – the boy had thanked him in later life.

The jury had a high proportion of smokers and they had to be regularly accommodated so, at mid-morning break, I met up again with Neil Summers. The pair of us headed downstairs to the gents' toilet, chatting away about Morris's testimony as we went. We went into the toilets and there, using the facilities, was the man himself.

There were only three urinals and he was standing at the middle one. There was only one thing for it – me and Neil took up position at the outer urinals and stood taking a leak on either side of our former teacher – the accused – in total silence. As Morris left, I motioned to Neil, silently urging him not to say anything; another wrong move would undoubtedly get me thrown out of the courtroom.

'It was strange seeing him after nearly thirty years,' Summers told me later. 'He was always intimidating, I was always scared of the guy; he had a menace about him. But when I saw him in court, he was just a pathetic little man.'

Back in court nine, Morris continued to give evidence, this

time dealing directly with the accusations against him. Over the course of his evidence and cross-examination, Morris would find a variety of flowery and extravagant ways of dismissing what his former pupils had said: it was all 'utterly laughable... risible fiction... fantasy to the power of ten... a fiction *tour de force*... a fantastic concoction of untruths.'

In the dock, he'd either claim to have no memory of the pupil in question or would say that the lad was simply lying. It was 'positively wicked' to suggest he'd touched one boy's genitals; in response to the accusation that he had a sexual interest in young boys, he stated, 'No, no, no. Never.'

Those involved in pursuing the case against Morris watched in fascination as he spoke. As well as taking note of anything he said that might contradict his previous statements, the police studied the way he was handling the situation.

'It all seemed a bit remote and fantastical to him that he should ever be sat there in court facing charges of sexual abuse,' DI Jed Pidd told me.

'I don't think he thinks he's done anything wrong,' said DC Nicola Graham. 'He's maintained his innocence throughout the investigation. I watched him give evidence at Manchester Crown Court, he didn't show a flicker of anything. He didn't show anything that showed he thought he was responsible for any of the allegations whatsoever. I've been in this unit many years and I've run many trials and it does happen. They convince themselves they've done nothing wrong.'

'I was shocked at the sheer arrogance that came across when he was giving evidence and the patronising way he spoke to me,' says prosecuting counsel Charlotte Crangle.

'You saw it in court. He wasn't doing himself any favours – using long words, technical terms about chemistry. He's obviously a very well-educated and intelligent man but he's got to appeal to a jury. You've got to sell yourself. He wasn't doing himself any favours.'

The language and tone of voice Morris used in the dock was extraordinary. It was as if he'd been briefed to use all the creepy trigger words of someone with a leering, unhealthy interest in young boys. Much was made of the different 'implements' used by him to beat 'naughty boys' with – not expressions I'd have advised him to use if I was on his defence team. I'd also have cautioned Morris against using the word 'weapon' when referring to the implements of punishment. He spoke at great length of how he'd tried various tools, like plimsolls, rubber hoses, his bare hand, the cane and the strap before settling on his weapons of choice.

In responding to the ex-pupils' accusations, Morris saved most of his disdain for Ground Zero. That boy, he told the court, was involved in the school plays and was an exceptionally gifted actor. He was also the class jester and, like jesters of old, was probably allowed a little more leeway than others. Morris claimed he had 'no memory' of the corporal punishment described by Ground Zero as taking place several times a week. What's more, the idea of putting carpet down Ground Zero's pants had, in fact, been the boy's – it was all a ruse to frighten the other pupils off from doing 'naughty things'.

While being questioned by the defence about his use of corporal punishment, Morris was asked about the wooden spoon he used to smack boys with. With a flourish, he produced a spoon from the inside pocket of his jacket. Had he used a spoon like that one to hit boys, he was asked?

No, he said, this was the very one he'd used all those years ago.' He'd clearly kept it as a souvenir.

'Until he pulled the spoon out, I had no idea that was going to happen,' Charlotte Crangle later told me. 'Usually, if the defence are going to show exhibits, they would show them to me beforehand so I have a chance to look at them, so they don't take me by surprise. But I didn't know he was going to come with the spoon he said he used to administer corporal punishment. The whole case I was trying to develop, and the picture I was trying to paint in court, was that it was all a very dramatic and theatrical performance when he was punishing a boy. That was the scenario he was getting his thrills from. That theatrical flourish added to my case.'

When Morris produced his spoon, I looked at the faces of the jury: *It can't just be me that thinks it's weird for a man to keep a bottom-smacking spoon for the best part of twenty years, can it?*

'The spoon?' remembers DC Barry Conway. 'No, I didn't know he was going to do that – it was a rabbit-out-the-hat moment. If that's what he felt he needed to do, so be it. It's his case.'

From the public gallery, Doctor Dad was, as ever, watching and taking notes. This was the parent who'd come to court thinking it was all a waste of time. Watching Morris in the dock, his view gradually began to change: 'I went into that courtroom with the knowledge that loads of lads all had a view of Morris as someone who dished out some pretty bad punishments and that they should steer clear of him. He could be pretty brutal when it came to corporal punishment. He had a generally creepy style. He was an extremely pompous person; he did his very best to belittle those he caught misbehaving.

'There wasn't a Damascene moment. I regard emotion as being destructive, not constructive. [But] I listened to the body of evidence, which was quite ragged. It didn't all fit together. Then Morris took the stand. In my view, his story was an elegantly-contrived, carefully-woven tapestry with a lot of holes in it that he would not spot because he showed no understanding of what the ordinary person would think about what he was saying. "The school had a reputation for theatricality and I was merely building on that when I said to the boy, 'Now whack yourself...'" and I'm thinking, *What a load of cock. The jury are going to think he's from the Planet Zog.*'

Though he denies there was one single moment that changed his mind, Doctor Dad had a simple but illuminating chat with one of the other parents: 'I spoke to one lad's mother,' he told me. 'Her face gave her away, and she said, "The damage that man has done to my son..." That was when I thought, *This is bigger, deeper and grimmer than I had ever appreciated.* The enormity of it began to get to me. It got stickier and stickier and stickier.'

Morris also told of his forbidden passion for Mahjid Mahmood, the man he claimed was the reason he held a stash of 'punishment porn' at Rivington Road. He said he had met Mahmood in 2006 and the pair engaged in sadomasochistic role play before sex – this was what aroused Mahjid and so it was why Morris had the material at his house. Despite his earlier denials, Morris was now admitting to downloading and viewing it but only to 'excite' Mahjid. Because of his religion and the fear of being ostracised by his Muslim community, Mahjid supposedly couldn't come forward to help, leaving Morris to fend for himself.

Another key element of Morris's defence was ex-pupils willing to speak on his behalf. Professional qualifications were well to the fore: Dr John Blackwell, Dr David Kitson, Matthew McGlennon, Dr Michael Gilmore, Michael Sarwar and Simon Delahunty all testified that the picture painted by the prosecution was not one they recognised.

It was bizarre to think that these men had experienced such a radically different schooling to the rest of us and felt able to give Morris their endorsement. One of the witnesses, Delahunty, was in my year and went through St Ambrose with me from the age of seven. I found it baffling. I saw Morris warmly embrace one of these old Ambrosians outside court nine.

There was much talk of what a great teacher Morris was. This wasn't news; even some of his victims said he was a very good teacher. His professional ability wasn't on trial.

'There seemed to be a divide between the people we had as victims and the ex-students he had as character witnesses,' said Charlotte Crangle. 'A divide between "A-stream" pupils and ones who weren't doing quite so well. So the favourites were the ones who came and spoke as to his good character. The victims were the ones who weren't favourites.'

There had been a moment of real disquiet when one of the character witnesses mentioned a 'briefing pack' they received from the defence team. Crangle was not best pleased.

'I wanted to ask these well-educated, professional men whether the pornography found at Morris's house – and I wanted to describe the pornography to them – affected their views of him, given they were here to give evidence as to his good character. [But] they knew about that and it stole my thunder.'

With all the evidence heard, it was time for both sides to make their closing statements – the last chance for both Crangle and McKee to summarise the case as they saw it.

Charlotte Crangle told the jury that Alan Morris was, indeed, a very good teacher but also a serial abuser. Those two things, she said, were not mutually exclusive. Morris used his power to sexually abuse boys via corporal punishment. The beatings were a cloak under which he hid and he picked on boys who he thought he could get away with abusing. He thrived on power and control and, when Morris was put in charge of discipline at St Ambrose, he had the perfect cover.

Crangle reminded the jury of the testimony the lads had given: the beatings, the touching, the way he made lads beat each other, the photos he took, the videos and computer material found at Rivington Road. Invoking the title of one of the videos at Morris's home, Crangle described Alan Morris as the 'Dirty Dean of Discipline'.

'Who is telling you the truth?' That was the question Hugh McKee put to the jury for the defence. He went though Morris's difficult childhood: the polio, the financial hardship, the difficulties with his brother's depression. Alan Morris was a very good teacher, McKee once again pointed out to the jury. He had helped pupils get to Cambridge – even some of

181

his victims praised his no-nonsense teaching style. Morris, he said, was a man dedicated to educating boys – but he had never been sexually attracted to them.

It took McKee considerably less time to get through his defence statement than it had taken Crangle to recap her points for the prosecution – a good sign, I thought.

Then Judge Timothy Mort spent a day and a half summing up the case for the benefit of the jury, backtracking through each charge and each victim – describing them to help the jury differentiate one ex-pupil from the other: 'he was the rather angry man in the suit... he was the man who now lives an almost hermit-like existence in Scotland... he was the rather nervous man...'

'The judge was extremely fair and that's all you want for both sides,' appraises DC Conway. 'He was down the middle and that's as it should be.'

The jury was then sent out to consider its verdict, with an information pack to help them keep track of the dizzying amount of testimony.

'By the time they came to retire and deliberate, it was three weeks or so since the first witness had given evidence,' acknowledges Charlotte Crangle. 'We did a timeline with a little photo of each victim – screenshots from their video interviews – with their name showing when they were at the school. Sometimes you need to be able to picture that person. It was one of the first documents in the jury bundle, one between two, that they're given with the indictment so they know the counts for each person; then there was a document showing how the equivalent school years work now for the younger members of the jury, copies of the defendant's interviews, the formal submission and photographs.'

By late morning on Wednesday, 16 July 2014 – midway through the fourth week of the trial – the jury was sent out to consider its verdicts. All we could do now was to wait. DC Nicola Graham pointed out that the jury in one recent historic trial – that of broadcaster Stuart Hall – returned its verdict in thirty minutes flat, so I was advised not to wander too far. It could all kick off at any time. But it didn't.

Boredom takes on new dimensions when you're sitting around in court waiting for a verdict. Any notion of tedium you held previously goes out of the window, bringing an ever more boring notion of boredom.

For the officers involved, it's just an endless opportunity to worry over every aspect of the case. 'You feel sick, it's horrible,' says Barry Conway. 'It's the worst part; that period of uncertainty is the worst feeling that you can have. I've been there and won and been there on occasions and lost, so I know how it feels to go through both. It's the loneliest place.'

I asked Barry to call it – an utterly pointless exercise but it helped pass the time. 'When it gets to the jury stage, my opinion doesn't really matter,' he said. 'It's down to these twelve people – that's what matters.' He was being as cautious as ever but, off the record, he seemed very quietly confident.

His colleague, Nicola Graham, didn't so much wear her heart on her sleeve as display it on a neon sign above her head. She would lurch from total confidence to fretful worry and back again in the space of a few minutes. For two days, she kept saying she was about to be sick.

'I'm human,' she explained to me, quite unnecessarily.

'We're all competitive in our own way and you want to win,' acknowledges Barry. 'You know how strong your case is, you know what you've got and, obviously, if it was down to you, he'd be found guilty and that's it. But it's just that uncertainty of it. You can never call it, no matter what anybody says.'

As we waited, we looked for something – anything – to distract ourselves. But no one could have predicted the incident that actually broke up the monotony.

The officers were waiting in the basement of the court when they got word that there was trouble potentially brewing at the side door. The former pupil whose evidence had been put aside early in the trial had returned to court to check if there had been a verdict yet. He was still upset about what happened and, what's more, very drunk.

'This was early doors too; we're talking mid-morning,' recalls Barry. 'We kept him downstairs and plied him with coffee. We sat him down and had a good long chat with him. We told him his evidence was a vital part to prove what we were dealing with. [It was] some compensation but not as much as he would have liked.'

Finally, late on Friday morning, the internal court PA system crackled into life with the words we'd been waiting for: everyone involved in the Alan Morris case was to return to court nine. There was a genuine kick-bollocks scramble up the stairs and a full-on push and shove to get through the crowd of people who'd been chucked out of number nine to accommodate us.

(Courts are busy places and are rarely left unused. While we were hanging about waiting, another case had taken up residence.)

We all took our places and were on our feet as Judge Mort made his return. It was a false alarm. He just wanted the barristers to know he needed to get off early that afternoon. If there was no news by three-ish, we'd need to have a rethink.

Back to the waiting game; hanging around the corridors and watching clocks tick. It was now close to the time when things would be closed down for the weekend. One rumour doing the rounds was that Morris hadn't brought an overnight bag and had left his car in the pay-and-display car park near Altrincham station – such was his belief that he'd be cleared and heading home to Rivington Road.

Then, just as we were getting close to 3pm and I'd pretty much given up, the tannoy kicked in again, telling us to return to court nine. Another false alarm? No, I was told... *this is it*.

We tumbled back in. There was an uncomfortably muggy atmosphere, like a changing room after a football match. I opened my notepad and wrote out the numbers one to nineteen to signify the charges Morris faced and put a circle around each number. I would write 'G' (guilty) or 'NG' (not guilty) next to each charge, depending on each individual verdict.

Alan Morris took his seat behind the security screen, put on his headphones and closed his eyes. Hugh McKee and Charlotte Crangle stared at their notes. DC Barry Conway was holding DC Nicola Graham's hand. DC Graham was holding my hand. She was *shaking*.

The general view among the cops was that the first charge might go against them – they were prepared for a 'not guilty'. But when the nominated foreman of the jury was asked for the first verdict, he said, 'Guilty.'

Only another eighteen to go.

Then I noticed something: the foreman didn't have a piece of paper. Either he had a memory of phenomenal proportions or all the verdicts were going to be the same.

And so it was. He said 'guilty' another eighteen times.

All of that warm, discomforting air in the room seemed to turn instantly cold. Nicola Graham had stopped shaking but started crying. Several members of the jury were in tears too. I mouthed 'Thanks' to them.

Alan Morris was perfectly motionless, his eyes still closed. The jury – looking washed-out and exhausted – was thanked by the judge for the way they had conducted both themselves and the case.

'To convict someone of offences of this nature is quite a brave thing for a jury to do,' Charlotte Crangle later told me. 'They've invested four weeks of their lives; they've lived and breathed the case as much as we have, so there's an emotional release when it's over. The whole enormity of the situation can make people emotional. But it's odd that you've got witnesses, police officers, jurors becoming more emotional than the defendant.'

There had been no mention of the Section 39 order, which had prevented any reporting of the case thus far. Was that going to stay in place? Were we allowed to talk openly about the trial now?

I asked Nicola Graham what the deal was and our chatter earned us a telling-off from a clerk, informing us to 'respect the court.' We managed to pass a note to Charlotte Crangle, who, in turn, put it to the judge.

Yes, the order would stay in place until the next trial. We were in the strange position of wanting to shout the result from the rooftops but not being allowed to.

So what now of Morris? It was made clear that, as a convicted sex offender, he was going to be remanded in custody until the next trial and that he was looking at a 'substantial term of imprisonment.'

Grim-faced defence counsel Hugh McKee asked the judge if Morris could be allowed a day or two to sort out his affairs and to make arrangements for the care of his brother. 'No,' said Judge Mort. Morris had talked about his mental-health issues during the trial and this meant he could be a suicide risk. He was going to jail right now.

I turned to look at Morris, to see if there was any final flicker of recognition as to what had just happened. But he'd gone. He'd been escorted out of the side door and was heading down to the prison van waiting to take him to Her Majesty's Prison, Manchester – better known as Strangeways.

The court was buzzing with talk, particularly about the imperturbable disconnect of Alan Morris from the proceedings; it was as if he was pretending the whole thing hadn't taken place.

'I'd heard he'd left his car at the tram stop and had both sets of keys with him,' says Charlotte Crangle. 'If I were defending him, obviously you advise them that, when the verdict comes

187

in, there's a chance you'll be remanded in custody, there's a chance that you'll turn up in the morning and you won't be going home that night, so you need to put some arrangements in place. We heard in court about his brother and how he was the carer for him. I don't know if he'd prepared him for the fact that he might not be coming home. You find, quite often, that defendants have convinced themselves of the story they've told over and over again – that it starts to become true.'

Speaking of the truth, what about Doctor Dad? He'd come into the trial convinced it was all a waste of time. But he'd spent nearly as much time watching the proceedings as I had.

'My view at the end was that the guy was guilty as charged,' he told me. 'All the intents were there. It was weight of evidence. The message that came over was the persecution, the betrayal of trust; there was just so much of it.'

Barry and Nicola had the phone numbers of all the lads stored in their mobiles. They immediately started ploughing though them, trying to tell them the news as soon as possible. I stood with Nicola as she rang one ex-pupil.

'Are you sitting down?' she asked. 'Guilty on all charges. He's on his way to prison.' I could hear muffled swearing from the person on the other end.

'I picked the phone up and, literally, when Nicola told me, I dropped it,' says Mike Bishop. 'I was just... *wow!* It was pretty overwhelming. I know it sounds so dramatic – it wasn't, it was just the way I was holding the phone! I quickly picked it up and said, "Are you fucking shitting me? Are you telling me the truth?" She said, "Yes." She sent me a text afterwards, thanking me. She's an absolute godsend. If more police officers were like her, the world would be a better place. I rang her back later. I'm guessing she was out with you [David Nolan] drinking because, when I phoned her back later, she was pissed. It was only six o'clock in the evening. But she did very well. She got very emotional, very happy. I genuinely think she cared about this as much as we did and that was superb. I had this overwhelming sense of relief and closure and resolution and that was just... powerful; it was a very, very, nice feeling.'

Nicola and Barry let me contact Ground Zero Boy. I knew it would be difficult to ring him at work, so I sent a text. The reply he sent, filled as it was with exclamation marks and swear words, suggested he was very pleased.

In between calls, Nicola pointed out, 'I owe you a hug,' reminding me of the deal we'd made in DI Pidd's office. So we hugged outside Minshull Street Crown Court. I started crying – again. Nicola joined me this time, which was kind of her.

When the calls were done, the police and the CPS team wasted very little time heading for Canal Street – the main thoroughfare of Manchester's gay village and the nearest bars to the court. They started ripping into the champagne, Barry had a pint of bitter, I had a Coke. My relationship with alcohol – which started back at St Ambrose in the 1970s – had turned nasty over the years and I quit boozing altogether in 2005.

After a while, I left them to it – I've got very limited patience when it comes to watching other people drink. But they deserved it. Still, it felt odd knowing that, because the Section 39 restriction was in place, no one knew that Morris had been found guilty except those directly involved. There would be no headlines in the papers; no lead story on the news. Nothing. The blackout would still be in place until at least the end of trial two. Morris was in jail – but hardly anyone knew about it.

That night, Manchester saw one of the biggest thunderstorms for years. Great chunks of lightning were accompanied by bone-rattling waves of thunder. I couldn't help but think of Alan Morris, lying in his bunk in Strangeways with horror-film atmospherics going on outside his window. I felt sorry for him.

Then I remembered his car, parked at Altrincham tram station. Not for a minute had it occurred to him that he might not be going home. It was a symbol of his total arrogance. His car probably had a ticket on it by now. It was about to collect a few more.

CHAPTER ELEVEN

BAD CHARACTER

Alan Morris came out of Strangeways prison and returned to Minshull Street court for the start of his second trial on Monday, 4 August 2014, just two weeks after the end of his first.

Behind the scenes, there had been much debate about whether it was worthwhile having trial number two at all. For many, the point had been made: Morris had already been found guilty nineteen times over. But there were still plenty of lads who wanted their day in court – a day they'd waited decades for.

The police who investigated the case felt that, in many ways, the job was done and were happy to stick with what they'd achieved. It's believed that Judge Timothy Mort agreed with them.

'It was a difficult thing,' says DI Jed Pidd. 'You never know what's in the judge's mind. Had we known, I think, perhaps, we would have argued more strongly that there was no need to go to trial two. But it was the CPS which put forward a convincing argument that we should.'

That argument boiled down to the fact that there was still a huge amount of evidence against Morris that hadn't been aired; it wasn't fair on the lads who'd had the guts to come forward not to bring their stories to court.

For the prosecution and defence teams, the police and Judge Mort, there must have been a strong whiff of déjà vu – but for the new jury's benefit, everything had to be laid out again as if the first trial had never happened.

Doctor Boy returned to tell of his experience at Rivington Road, to set the scene for ten other lads and their evidence. Once again, the prosecution case was put forward that Morris's use of corporal punishment had crossed the line into indecent assault. The new jury would hear the tales of the Dark Room, the Paddywhack and families too concerned about losing assisted places to complain. But there were new twists to follow too.

One victim told the court he was inspired by Morris to study chemistry at Cambridge and even dedicated his thesis to his ex-teacher. It wasn't until later in life that he fully realised how the things that had gone on in the chemistry lab at St Ambrose were wrong. The witness claimed Morris had forced the boy's head between his legs, touched and pinched his bottom in front of a class of boys and forced him and another boy to spank each other in the Dark Room.

The ex-pupil also told of an incident during a school play

when Morris asked him to take his car keys out of his trouser pocket for him, ostensibly because he had stage make-up on his hands.

'Looking back, there seemed to be no obvious reason for the defendant to need his keys at that time,' Charlotte Crangle told the jury. 'This didn't occur to [the ex-pupil] and he just did as he was told; reached into the defendant's trouser pocket for the keys. Mr Morris had an expression of satisfaction on his face when this had been done and merely asked him to put the keys on the side.'

Another ex-pupil told how he would be beaten on a weekly basis, claiming that sometimes Morris would touch his backside to make sure he had nothing hidden 'down there' to protect him from a beating. He alleged he was left in the Dark Room, bent over a stool, as Morris walked around him, rubbing his groin on his head as he passed. He also claimed Morris forced boys to cane each other and tried to make him strip naked for 'changing practice' when he was late from games. The boy finally reacted, saying to Morris that he planned to tell the police about what had gone on. He didn't and the matter was hushed up, despite Morris claiming he'd have the boy thrown out of St Ambrose.

Another former Ambrose lad told how Morris gave him the Paddywhack on the backside on a weekly basis, sometimes every other day. Again, he alleged Morris touched him to check he had no padding in his pants and interfered with his clothing.

'There was never an option to receive the punishment to the hand as with other teachers,' Charlotte Crangle told the court.

'And with every blow delivered, the defendant expected [the pupil] to say, "Thank you, sir," although he never did. This was happening on a regular basis and often caused difficulties at home, as [the pupil] did not want his parents to see the red marks or bruises caused and question him about them. He did not feel able, at the time, to say anything, due to his embarrassment and his fear of the defendant. [Morris] even resorted to making derogatory sexual remarks about [the pupil's] mother on one occasion, which served to reinforce [the pupil's] insecurities and ensured he would not say anything at home.' Stricken with anxiety and panic attacks, the boy left the school and went to a local college to continue his studies.

Another ex-pupil who attended the school throughout the 1980s claimed he was offered the choice between twelve hits on the backside with his trousers on or one smack on the bare backside. Charlotte Crangle outlined his other claims:

'The defendant would take a piece of chalk and mark an "X" on one buttock cheek and refer to the Paddywhack as his friend. He would then deliver a number of blows – six – to the cheek with the chalk on it and then make anther mark on the other cheek and repeat the process. He would call this "X marks the spot". [The pupil] could tell that he was enjoying this and taking some kind of sadistic pleasure from the whole performance.'

Yet another ex-pupil claimed that, in the late 1980s, he and other pupils were told to make noises as if they were in pain, while hitting each other with the Paddywhack. Morris allegedly pulled out their shirts to expose the tops of their backsides beforehand. Photographs were sometimes taken and

– in an echo of what happened to Ground Zero Boy ten years earlier – it was claimed the boy was asked to put a 'figure-of-eight shaped' piece of foam down his pants before being hit. This witness told the court that, in later life, he was due to get married at Holy Angels Church and had to specifically ask for Deacon Morris not to be involved.

Another pupil from the 1980s told how he was asked to sign an index card stating that he'd agreed to being punished with the Paddywhack; this card was then placed into what Morris referred to as the 'naughty-boy box'. The witness told the jury that Morris would single out about five boys in every year for regular punishments – and that he was one of them.

Another lad recalled being asked to put foam down his pants so he could be beaten in front of younger boys, in order to frighten them; it was either that or a full-on beating. He agreed to go along with the theatrical demonstration.

One ex-pupil told a familiar tale of how he'd complained to his mother about being picked on by Morris, claiming the teacher was beating him in the Dark Room and telling him to cry out in pain – as well as taking photographs and getting him to beat other boys while he watched. Anyone familiar with the first trial would recognise these themes but there was another aspect that rang bells from the previous case, as outlined by Charlotte Crangle: '[The ex-pupil] had, in fact, told his mother about the defendant's conduct towards him while he was still at the school but she feared that she would not be taken seriously and did not want to jeopardise her son's assisted place there [and] so did not approach the school at the time. Morris didn't teach [the pupil] but singled him out for punishment on a very regular basis – sometimes once or twice a week, or [at] other times every few months.'

Nervous Boy and David Prior also gave evidence in trial two, telling the jury about their experiences at the hands of Morris. Their feelings about appearing before the jury were contrasting, to say the least.

Nervous Boy had been on holiday the day before he was due to give evidence but had been severely delayed on his return home. 'I ended up getting back home at 3am,' he told me. 'And I was due in court at 9.30am. I ended sitting up half the night – I'd been drinking coffee all the way home, so I was wired. So I sat there going, *I can't believe it. What am I doing here? This is the night I should have gone to bed at 8pm!*'

He also recalls 'staring and staring' at Morris when he entered court nine: 'I wasn't scared about looking at him but also I didn't want to be obsessed with it. I wanted to focus on the questions that were being asked and looking at the jury and the judge; I didn't want it to be about me and him, really. I wanted it to be about the evidence I gave. My strongest feeling was that I wanted it to be a cathartic process. I would rid myself, as much as I could, of this stuff that'd been sitting inside me, that I'd never spoken to anybody about. So, when I actually got to court – I'd never been in a court before – I felt much better. I looked at him and thought, *There's nothing you can do to me anymore; I've got a family, I've got a life to live here and I'm not going to let this eat away at me. I'm just going to get on with my life.*'

David Prior told how he'd been singled out despite being a model pupil: Morris would pick him up and turn him upside down; get him to pose for photos in strange positions and smack him with a chalk-tipped ruler that left a mark on his trousers.

David told me he had actually been looking forward to appearing in court nine: 'It's a weird thing to say but I kind of enjoyed it. In the sense that here's the one man in my life who I'd not had a grain of sympathy for, or at least a hell of a lot of fear of. But now I just felt, *I'm not afraid of you anymore. I'm a grown man with children. You're having your come-uppance here*, which was long overdue, and I felt happy that I was contributing to this. I would have felt much, much worse if I was watching all the reports and I hadn't contributed in some way. I intensely disliked the man – there was no sympathy from me at all.'

On top of the new testimonies, the prosecution was allowed to give the new jury a devastating piece of evidence: Alan Morris had already been convicted of nineteen charges startlingly similar to the ones they were hearing. This was classified as evidence of his 'bad character' – something of an understatement, in my view, but compelling information that certainly seemed to indicate he was guilty of yet more offences.

Midway through the trial, one officer told me they were delighted by the way things were going – they couldn't really have been panning out any better. Discussions were even taking place about trial three. As ever though, DC Barry Conway was cautious.

'It's never a walk in the park when you go to trial,' he told me. '[But] the evidence was the same as the first, presented in the same way, by equally intelligent and eloquent people, and the added strength of that case was the "bad character". That's presented by the means of a formal admission by the prosecution, which was agreed by the court with the judge – that he had already been found of guilty of nineteen offences in relation to former pupils at St Ambrose and that related to fifteen indecent assaults and also gross indecencies.'

After giving his evidence, David Prior felt confident that a conviction for Morris on trial two was 'never in doubt' because of 'the number of witnesses, the status of the witnesses, the fact we all had similar stories but obviously hadn't colluded and also – from my personal experience of being in court – because of the pitiful performance of the defence barrister. He was obviously just clutching at straws. At one point, the jury was laughing at something he was trying to assert about my statement. And I thought, *This is only going one way.*'

As well as the evidence from alleged victims and witnesses, former pupils Matthew McGlennon and Dr Michael Gilmore returned to speak on Morris's behalf – they were joined by Professor John Morrill and Professor Eamonn Duffy, former Cambridge University lecturers and friends of Morris. Things were moving quickly – trial two seemed to be a swifter affair than its predecessor; there was a feeling of getting the job done, of matters being dealt with, of business being tidied up.

Midway through week three, the jury was sent out to consider their verdicts. After a day, Judge Timothy Mort called them back to gently remind them he would accept a majority decision – if ten out of twelve agreed, he'd accept that as a verdict. They continued with their deliberations.

Towards the end of the week, he asked them if they were

making progress. The jury reported back that they had reached verdicts on five of the charges but couldn't reach a conclusion on the remainder. The judge asked whether, if they were to be given more time, they would be able to reach verdicts on the other charges. But the jury was stuck and extra time wouldn't make it come unstuck.

They returned to court nine and the judge announced it was going to be a case of a hung jury. He thanked the members and sent them home. Several jury members were seen shaking their heads in disbelief. Alan Morris was led away and returned to Strangeways – he was still a convicted sex offender awaiting sentence. Trial two had ended with a hung jury – the chances now of a third trial were very slim indeed.

Some of the officers who'd worked on the case were shaking their heads too. 'I just don't know. It's one of these inexplicable things,' says DC Conway. 'We obviously didn't convince the jury enough to find him guilty in that second trial. If you asked me would I change anything, no, I wouldn't. Would I do anything differently? No, I wouldn't. Because I think it was run the same as the first trial was run. But that's the uncertainty of the process sometimes and it's all down to those twelve people and convincing at least ten of them of the guilt of that person.'

'Yes, we did think there was a good chance that he'd be found guilty,' admits DC Graham, 'but nothing surprises me with the twelve-person jury decision. You can't underestimate the decisions of a jury, can you? And you've two separate trials and two separate groups of people – slightly different evidence, [although] we did have the bad character to go with it. We don't know what the voting was. We don't get to hear – it's one of the questions you ask yourself forever. You get nine people who agree and think he's guilty and three that don't and that one person makes a massive difference.'

'A hung jury is like a score draw,' explains prosecutor Charlotte Crangle. 'It doesn't mean he is not guilty. The charges lie on file; they're still there if anything was to be resurrected in the future. They're not acquittals, they're not convictions, they are just there.'

One theory the detectives discussed is that the jury didn't fully connect the corporal-punishment aspect of the case with the sexual side – whereas the two had been intrinsically linked in trial one. Could the police, the CPS, all those involved, in fact, have done more to secure guilty verdicts?

'You always ask yourself that question,' says DI Pidd. 'The truth is that the people who were working on it throughout left no stone unturned. There was no other evidence we could have got and I think Charlotte Crangle presented the evidence in a highly convincing way. Truthfully, I don't think we could have done anything better. But we were always going to struggle on that point of the association that made it sexual assault, as opposed to just an assault.'

'The witnesses were just as good the second time around,' confirms Crangle. 'They knew about all his convictions from the first trial, they knew about the bad character evidence, that all went in without argument. In the first trial, a lot of the accounts were more overtly sexual. I think that's what the jury struggled with. Sometimes you wonder if they've been listening to the same evidence that we have. It's really hard.

It's a random generation of twelve people who come from every walk of life. You never know what experiences a juror may have had that affect their perceptions of the case. You never know.'

'The problem with the Alan Morris trial from the outset has been to unpick physical abuse from sexual abuse,' concurs Jed Pidd. 'Physical abuse was far more acceptable in those days than it is now. So there was a context of that being more OK. Therefore, if we were just taking this man to court around physical abuse, he was unlikely to get found guilty. What we always had to prove is that physical abuse was a concoction that allowed him to become sexually aroused – I think that was the key point in both trials. In trial one, we managed to convince a jury that was absolutely the case. In the second trial, we were asking the jury to take a greater leap of faith around that and the links between the two were more tenuous and more difficult to establish, in the minds of the jury. I think they came back and said they weren't convinced and, on these, they just couldn't make a decision.'

Despite the setback, all concerned were convinced it was still the correct decision to go for the second trial. 'One hundred per cent right,' says Barry Conway. 'People wanted their day in court. Plus I think it had to be out there, the full extent of what Morris had done. Plus there's his reluctance to admit guilt. Just to have left it at the first trial would have been wrong. I think it was the right decision... just the "wrong" second result.'

Nicola Graham, as ever, took it personally: 'I felt quite low really,' she told me. 'But I've had many low moments where

I've lost trials in the past. You really have to get used to it and deal with it. What kept us going really was that we knew we'd won anyway and this was the icing on the cake. We'd got the cake the month before, in July. So we had to refocus and know [that], the following week, he was going to get sentenced.'

'We knew after the first trial that there probably wasn't a great deal of point in the second trial,' says DI Pidd. 'However, when we spoke to CPS colleagues, I thought they had a really good point, which was, "How can we go to all these victims and say, 'Look, we're sentencing this prolific paedophile on a third of the cases that could go to court'?" We need two thirds of the cases to say, "There is no longer a public interest for these cases going to court [for a third time]." Now at the end of trial two, albeit we had a hung jury, two thirds of the people that had reported their sexual abuse to us had been to court and told their stories.'

As people filed out of court nine, the police had the task of ringing the ex-pupils who'd given evidence and telling them the news. The mood in which this was done was a marked contrast to the elation I saw after trial one.

'They were upset, obviously,' says DC Barry Conway. 'They couldn't understand why he wasn't found guilty – there was a mixture of emotions. As the officer in the case, [you're in] a lonely place. It's just a horrible job to have to do.'

When Barry Conway rang Nervous Boy, he was on holiday: 'I knew it probably wasn't going to be the greatest of news because Barry took a lot longer to tell me than he had when it was really good news. But, eventually, he got round to saying that the jury couldn't come to a verdict, it was a hung jury, which I think totally confused me really. Then you start thinking, *What did I do wrong? It must have been my evidence.* It's one of those things. I just got on with the rest of my holiday. I thought, *Sod it.*'

David Prior also received the call and took the news badly: 'It never crossed my mind that it would end in the way it did,' he told me. 'I just thought it was never in doubt. More than anything else, because of the personal experience I've had of the man, it genuinely has shaken my trust in the justice system.'

'Nicola phoned me,' recalls Doctor Boy. 'I was angry. Devastated. I work with normal human beings and I know they can be notoriously unpredictable. Juries – what can you say? It's their decision. You have to stand in front of your peer group and that's how we judge life. But I was frustrated and angry about it because I thought – particularly as the information about the first case was known to them – it was a no-brainer. It must have been difficult to ignore that. Because we'd had such a great result on the first trial, I was frustrated about the second. Those poor lads hadn't had their justice, in a way. The guys from the third trial wouldn't get theirs either. I felt sorry for the lads who pitched up and did their best but the jury were unconvinced.'

There would be no champers on Canal Street this time around. Team spirits were running low. There was the possibility of a retrial but no one's heart seemed to be in it. Besides which, even if the trial was run again and Morris was found guilty, it was unlikely he'd receive a hugely increased sentence, as he was already tapping on the ceiling of the available prison tariff. As far as a third trial was concerned? Forget it.

But, if this was it, there was a slight relief in some quarters that the whole thing was over. The police and some of the CPS team felt that Morris himself wanted the trials to carry on as long as possible – they suspected he was enjoying watching ex-pupils talk about what had happened to them; getting off on it.

As for me, well, part of me thought, *What with all the new evidence, plus the knowledge of the nineteen guilty verdicts in trial one, how could it happen?* I'd been told, way off the record, that even the defence team was shocked. But, if the idea of following the case was to show how things worked – how they can go right or wrong – the result certainly highlighted how bringing historical cases to trial and securing a conviction is a tricky business. There are no guarantees.

Another part of me – the cynical old journalist – also thought, *There's a plot twist for the book that no one would be expecting...*

CHAPTER TWELVE

VERY
CHILLY INDEED

Having spent so much time sitting in an empty press gallery in court nine, it was a little odd to be told, 'Get into court early or you won't get a seat.'

There were so many journalists on Thursday, 28 August 2014 (the day Judge Timothy Mort was going to sentence Alan Morris) that some members of the press were asked to sit in the empty jury section. The Section 39 order, which had banned any mention of the trial and its contents, was about to be lifted, so a field day was about to be had.

As they all filed in, I felt a pit peeved, if I'm honest: *Where were you lot during the last few months of evidence and cross-examination?* There was one consolation though: I'd been filming with Nicola and the team throughout the trial, interviewing Ground Zero Boy and other ex-pupils for a special investigation into St Ambrose, which was going to air on ITV Granada that night. It would include my confronting Alan Morris outside court and reconstructions we'd filmed at a school in East Manchester.

Funds were tight during that shoot, so I'd had to play Morris myself. My thirteen-year-old son, Scott, also appeared as one of the victims. It was an odd day all round. Nicola and I had pre-recorded an interview with presenter Tony Morris (no relation) about how we'd worked together during the case. Thanks to the head of news, Lucy West, *Granada Reports* (where I'd worked many years earlier) was going to give half its programme over to a St Ambrose historical-abuse special, fronted by me. So I knew that, whatever the journalists scurrying around court were able to pull together, my piece was going to smash theirs to bits.

(It's childish, I know, but it made me feel better.)

As well as the journalists, there were parents, witnesses, victims, old Ambrosians and police officers streaming into court. Doctor Boy was there and so was Doctor Dad. Jed, Barry and Nicola were obviously in attendance. Court nine was buzzing.

Just a few days earlier, the decision had been made not to go for a re-run of trial two, so there definitely wouldn't be a trial three. Judge Mort had indicated he wanted to sentence Morris pretty sharpish, so this morning in court had been organised in haste.

Two years after Doctor Boy made his *faux pas* in the American Bar & Grill, thirteen years after Ground Zero had contacted police, thirty-three years after I'd left St Ambrose and forty-two years since Alan Morris had joined the school, it was the end of the line.

Journalists and police officers are cut from very similar cloth, so the detectives and I kicked off an informal guessing game about how many years Morris would get. It was complicated by the fact that the law was different when the offences took place, so an educated guess was tricky.

'When we looked at sentencing I really didn't have a clue,' DC Barry Conway recalls. 'The judges have guidelines set down with the Law Lords of what is an appropriate sentence. I just didn't know because of some recent convictions, like Max Clifford and Stuart Hall: Clifford got quite a few years and Hall didn't. I'm always on the pessimistic side anyway. I thought we were looking at maybe three, four years.'

Then Alan Morris appeared. He did not give the people in the packed court so much as a glance. He sat down, put on the loop headphones so he could hear what was going on and, as ever, rested his chin on the crook of his walking stick and closed his eyes. His hair looked shorter than the last time I'd seen him and he wasn't wearing a tie – the first time I think I'd ever seen him without one. The informality of it seemed odd. Then I remembered he was considered a suicide risk...

I sat with Doctor Boy. He'd been there at the start and he was here for the final act. Like all the lads, he'd very much existed in isolation during the trial – now he was surrounded by like-minded souls.

'It was nice to see some wild faces in the gallery,' he told me. 'The two guys behind me were very distressed. There were some very grim-faced parents. The gallery was packed, though I didn't know a lot of these people. And you know what? Morris, the cheeky bastard, didn't even look up. He sat there with his chin on his stick. He didn't open his eyes once to acknowledge the judge, the jury, the journalists and, most of all, the public gallery. *How fucking dare you not even cast one glance over to those lads? You ignorant, arrogant man!* That's disgusting. And I looked across at him a lot because I wanted to catch just one glance, just to say, *You know and I know. All these other lads in the public gallery know. But you won't even look up. How dare you. That's insulting!'*

Doctor Dad was there too: 'I looked at Morris and thought, *How desperately sad.* I didn't have any sense that I needed revenge. I think it's a dangerous emotion. But, in the end, I thought he was a sad monster. *What neurons have misfired in your brain in order for you to want to damage other people to seek gratification for yourself?'*

Impact statements from the victims were made available to the judge: these were questionnaires the lads had been asked to fill in about how being at the school and being involved in the case had affected them, any personal views on Morris himself, and what, if any, opinion they held on sentencing.

Paul Wills later told me that his statement 'took about two hours to write but about ten years to think about.' It follows below:

I know full well that the school, and Morris with it, changed me for the worse and it's no easy task to separate the two. Gone was a boy who loved his books, chatted freely to anyone and had the ambition and intelligence to be a vet. I'd left the school with relief thinking I'd survived well enough but really I think myself and many others left as beaten dogs, very wary and very cautious. Patterns of behaviour evolve and become established and in my case at least they're harmless enough and carry no consequences for anyone else. I've avoided any situation in work and general life where I'm either a boss or the bossed, and that is a certain and sure route to isolation. The last twelve years I've lived on a mountainside, a life most people would consider brutally basic, but one I welcomed. My social life is three border collies – a good night out for me is clambering up a mountain whilst my dogs chase their shadows and track the scent of foxes and deer. Ambitions for me are moving further north; less people, more space. I don't say any of this expecting sympathy or worse, pity, as I count myself lucky to be here. From time to time, particularly in the long cold winter I've wondered a little bit how I ended up here and then I duck the obvious answers by getting busy with something mundane. But the last year and a half have been an unpleasant time, where dwelling in the past has been more or less inevitable. Schools like St Ambrose are well and truly of the past and I think most people will be glad of that, I consider this trial very necessary not least because Morris, right up to the time of his arrest, had access to the school through his position as deacon at Holy Angels. Despite the widespread knowledge of who and what Morris was, the Catholic Church allowed him to remain within a few yards of the prep school where the eight-year-old boys begin their St Ambrose education. I hope the Church answers some straight questions about how this came to be, but I doubt that they will. This school, that now wishes to accept children from the age of five, would do well to consider their ability to manage the welfare of the children entrusted to their care. Morris is not a distant figure in the school's murky past but a figure many staff and students encountered daily as recently as October 2012. I hope the school acknowledges this mistake on their part, but I doubt that they will.

This is Mike Bishop's statement:

Since this investigation started my life has been horrendous. I have had huge relationship problems, as I could not speak to my family about what happened, and this alienated them. I have had my partner of sixteen years leave me on two occasions because of my inability to deal with the way I felt. I have sought independent counselling (through work) as this was the only way to talk to someone that was unable to judge me for what happened. I am having approximately two sessions (one hour each) a month. This has helped but the situation and experience is still very raw.

This has been a torrid time in my life and his actions 25 years ago have really impacted [upon] me growing up as I have huge trust issues in life. I had managed to place this experience at the back of my mind, the trial needed to happen, but it has opened that box again and I am 12 years of age again. It's a very difficult time, and my reaction to the verdict told me that I had not even started to deal with the pain that he caused me. I am very happy that justice has been done, and I am happy that he will pay for what he did to me. Thankfully, as my life has never been what it could have been, and he is to blame for a large part of this, I am comforted that I now know his life will change for the worse.

Derek Scanlan's statement:

There was a general culture of violence at St Ambrose. This led to a constant state of anxiety which impacted on learning. It also made me depressed. Without school I tried to get away from everyone to be alone as much as possible. I didn't trust adults, had no respect for authority – only fear of it.

At the time, I felt I couldn't tell my parents. The school made me feel guilty and ashamed. I felt I must be doing something wrong. There was no compassion within the school. When I left to go to sixth-form college I genuinely couldn't believe how pleasant life could be without the violent environment of St Ambrose. From my achievements later in life I am certain that I should have achieved better academic results at school and St Ambrose had a negative impact on my education.

Morris took the violent abuse at the school to another level. The school environment meant that there was no accountability for his actions. There was no one to report it to. He knew that, which gave him the power to bully and abuse. He made me do things that I was ashamed of, that I do not want to remember, or have to continue to think about. He contributed to making my childhood a place of fear and humiliation.

As an adult, I've tried my best to put these experiences behind me and on the whole have been able to overcome them, with my own inner resources. However, in recent years I started training for a job with the fire service. The regime of authority, orders, uniforms and commands needed as part of the fire service took me back to bad childhood experiences at St Ambrose and old emotions resurfaced. I felt stressed, anxious and depressed and had to leave. This was highly embarrassing and difficult to explain to friends and colleagues. It meant that I couldn't contribute a valuable service to my local community and that I had to give up a long-term employment opportunity. A number of years ago I underwent a course of hypnotherapy at Glasgow Dental School for tooth grinding due to anxiety.

If any one of the multiple violent actions that happened on a daily basis to me at St Ambrose happened to anyone, let alone children, it would not be tolerated today. I also wonder if it would have been tolerated then outside the closed society of St Ambrose.

Being involved in the investigation has been stressful. Emotions and traumatic experiences that I have tried to put behind me in order to live a normal life have resurfaced. The build-up to the trial and months of waiting have left time to dwell on these childhood experiences. Having to give evidence at the trial was a very daunting and an intense experience, particularly as the abuser was there. It meant going into detail about horrible incidents that I've never wanted to relate to anyone else. I had to do this in front of a room full of people. I felt that Morris was enjoying the experience. It made me angry. How does he have the audacity to be such an unrepentant liar? He shouldn't be able to have any further access to harm children, which is why I was willing to give evidence against him.

I only have knowledge of the crimes he committed against me and my friends. I do not know the detail of the other charges against him. I therefore don't feel in a position to give views on the sentence that he should receive. However, he would appear not to accept the consequences of his actions. It is unimaginable that he has wanted to make his victims go through the court proceedings. I felt that he was attempting to abuse me again by making me appear in court, but he had forgotten that over thirty years has passed and I am no longer the vulnerable eleven-year-old boy that he exposed to indecent and violent acts.

The police, the CPS and witness support volunteers have all been really helpful as have my local police in Stornoway. I have been grateful for their support. I also appreciate that the judge kept the case very focused. It was useful and a relief that there was a ban on media coverage during the case.

When the call went out for witnesses to crimes at the school I had to report what had happened to myself and my peers as I didn't want Morris to be able to abuse any more children. My only regret is that I didn't report these crimes much earlier so that I could have saved others from being abused by him.

Then there was Ground Zero, the 'lively kid' who'd tried and failed to get the police to charge Alan Morris in 2001. The one who had stood up first and then had to wait for thirteen years while the wheels of justice started, stopped and then began to move again. This is his statement:

I've been treated with compassion and respect during the investigation by both the police and court officials throughout the proceedings and guided comfortably through the process, for which I'm very grateful. At the same time I resent the humiliation of having to publicly discuss what happened at St Ambrose and having the case on my mind for months and having to recall the events there again. And knowing a defence lawyer was going to do exactly what Alan Morris does which is to say it's not true. Involvement in the case has been a very disturbing time. However, I'm glad to have given my evidence and had my experience at St Ambrose recognised. I don't have any comment about how long the defendant's sentence should be, I'm glad that's a matter of law because I prefer not to judge any punishment. My reason for testifying and my aim with coming forward has been solely to have him stopped from doing anything else to anyone. Thank you very much to Barry Conway and Nicola Graham for their support throughout this process. My opportunity to study and form healthily as a person was totally trashed at St Ambrose and I was only ever going to take a step to a decent future once I was out of there. What went on with Mr Morris ruined that environment. He was my subject tutor, form teacher and mentor and he abused that position and abused me. One thing that can still make me weep, at age forty-nine, is Alan Morris.

Sitting next to Doctor Boy, I watched his expression change as the judge went through the experiences of each of the victims. His face became pale. He turned to look at me with mouth wide open. It sounds like the kind of description that writers chuck around without thinking about it but *it really was*.

'Fucking hell,' he whispered.

'Now do you realise why it was so important that you came forward?' I asked.

'I hadn't heard a lot of the information,' he later told me. 'But when the judge summarised it all and read out the victim impact statements, at least three of those boys suffered significantly; some of their lives had been massively affected, possibly even destroyed; their prospects destroyed, the way they hold themselves in life has been destroyed. That is a deeply unpleasant thing to hear. To listen to that is heartbreaking. No sexual abuse has an impact on nobody. I felt a bit angry about listening to those guys' statements.'

Judge Timothy Mort began his final speech – the section that would interest the journalists in attendance. It's the bit that gets quoted in the press, where the judge gives his overview of the case and, hopefully, provides some harsh and telling soundbites about the defendant.

Initially, Mort spoke about Alan Morris's good deeds, his excellence as a teacher – 'strict and talented' – and the difficulties he'd faced early in life. Then his tone changed. Addressing Morris directly, he described the ex-teacher as 'resolute in your denial' of the accusations against him. He said Morris had escaped justice for so long because he had ruled with fear as he handed out the punishments, with many boys believing they had done something wrong – whether that was the case or not – and, subsequently, not telling their parents.

Morris saw himself as above everyone, including the school governors; he'd exhibited a 'shocking degree of abuse of trust' and had been 'incredibly arrogant.' The trial, Mort said, had been an 'emotional ordeal for the victims that unlocked painful memories,' adding, 'Many families who were devout Catholics felt the teachers could do no wrong. It is also clear that you calculated [that], by becoming head of discipline, you had the respect of the head [teacher] and, with disdain for the governors, you were really confident you could act above the law.' Mort also commended Nicola Graham and Barry Conway for their work and, in particular, the way they'd dealt with the lads.

Then Judge Timothy Mort did something I really wasn't expecting: he mentioned *me*. Harking back to the incident outside court when I'd confronted Morris, he said, 'It is clear that [the victims] were telling the truth and it is an interesting observation that, during this trial, I had cause to rebuke one of them, who went up to you and said, "Remember the school motto, which loosely translates as 'Dedicate your life to the truth'?" It seems at least the pupils were loyal to the motto of their old school.'

I could feel lots of eyes looking at me. For once, I managed not to cry, though it was a close thing (real progress, I think you'll agree).

'The judge obviously acknowledged what you said to Morris, about the pupils telling the truth and that he wasn't,' said DC Nicola Graham. 'When he actually said it in court, I got quite moved... I thought it was quite a nice part of his summing up; really quite cool of him – professional and sensitive.'

Then Judge Mort started to go through each of the victims and the offences and gave his sentence on each one. Morris had been charged and tried under the 1956 Sexual Offences Act but the judge would also be taking into account the current sentencing guidelines under the 2004 act. In other words... this was anyone's guess.

The names and numbers started to fly around, so I used my fingers to try to keep tally. Some of the sentences were to run concurrently, so they didn't add to the total. I thought I was on top of it, then an ex-pupil leaned over and asked me, 'What are we up to so far?' and I lost track.

The judge seemed to have been especially shocked by the incident with the lad who came to return some schoolbooks. When Morris had found that not all the books were accounted for, he ordered the teenager to drop his pants and he beat him, removing his own trousers in the process and pushing his erection against the boy's bare backside while fondling him. Morris would receive an additional three years for that offence.

Then he gave the final total: nine years.

Nine years. It was a surprise, even to Charlotte Crangle.

'If I'm honest, it was slightly higher than I thought,' she said. 'But not outside the bounds of what was going to happen. The judge did it very carefully.'

It appears the historical nature of the offences placed the sentence Morris received at the higher end of the tariff. Remember, he had been charged under the old laws and was being sentenced with one eye on the 1956 Act.

'Because these were indecent assaults on males, the maximum then was ten years,' Charlotte later explained to me. 'If they'd been females, it wouldn't have been as much. It wouldn't matter now.'

'When we got the nine years, for me, that was a great result,' said DC Barry Conway. 'I don't know the guidelines but I think the judge gave him the maximum he possibly could and I think it was appropriate. I think anything else would have been an insult to me and all the people who came forward.'

'Any sense of disappointment from the second trial was wiped out by that sentence of nine years,' said DI Jed Pidd. 'I would have been really, really disappointed if we'd gone to trial one and got such a convincing "yes, he's guilty", gone to trial two and got this wishy-washy result and then got what I would have regarded as a piddling sentence which didn't reflect the seriousness of what had gone on. He got a sentence which reflected the fact he bullied and abused kids in the most awful way and those poor children had nowhere to go. They were completely at his mercy for years on end, physical and sexual abuse day after day after day; they were living out his fantasies for him and they had no choice whatsoever in that. They've been mentally scarred for years and years afterwards, with some still not able to lead fulfilling lives, still not able to have fulfilling relationships. All because Mr Morris wanted to get a hard-on at their expense.'

As Morris was led away through the side door of the court, I wondered if someone might say or call out something that summed up what we were feeling.

One lad behind me finally broke the silence. 'Bye bye!' he said in a loud, sarcastic voice. It was a strangely childish thing to say – the kind of comment a schoolboy might make.

Then it was done. We filed out of court nine for the final time, clumping together in small groups in the waiting area, not quite sure what to do with ourselves. After trial one, credit cards had been whipped out and champagne had been bought on Canal Street. Now it seemed like the last thing anyone wanted to do.

Doctor Boy – who'd started the second wave of action against Morris after telling his story to the police – seemed strangely deflated by the whole experience.

'I'm not a vindictive individual. It's been sad for everyone,' he told me as we mooched about the corridors and walkways of Minshull Street court. 'It's a sad episode. Justice has been done, a lot of lads have gotten some closure but a lot of the lads still need help. I don't know how I feel. I don't know if anything makes it better. I'm not sure it's that cathartic – he's injured some people, we've injured him. Has anyone won anything?'

Charlotte Crangle had certainly won her case but she, too, became aware of a strange sadness that seemed to envelop the lads. Morris had been jailed but there was little by way of celebration.

'They seemed to feel like, *Yes, we've gotten revenge on him*, but does that still leave a sour taste in the mouth?' she said when I asked about the muted reaction among the ex-pupils. 'In their heads, they had this memory of him being this big, tall, domineering, imposing man. Now they're adults and they're seeing him with his walking stick, using the hearing-loop system in the dock. Going to prison isn't a nice way to live out your days – but that's to their credit that they could be so Christian [as] to think like that. It's common decency.'

At his remote home in Scotland, Paul Wills displayed a similar decency when he was rung with the news. 'What a sad man,' he told me. 'What a waste. I think jail is a waste of time. If the judge had said, "I'm going to tag you, you can't go near children for the rest of your life," I wouldn't have minded. I'd have made him work – he can mark chemistry papers for 10p an hour.'

'I had mixed emotions really,' Nervous Boy told me. 'I was a bit shocked by the length of the sentence. I didn't think he would get anything like that, to be honest. There was an element in me that felt sorry for him really. It's hard to rationalise. I was glad he was found guilty and I think the length of the sentence is immaterial to me really. I do sort of hope that he gets some help. I hoped he'd find some peace in himself, some way of reconciling it to himself and admitting he's done wrong, as he spent most of the time in complete denial of it. When you think about it, Morris was my first sexual experience – not ideal is it?'

'I never thought he would make it to prison,' said ex-pupil Scott Morgan. 'I thought he'd just kill himself. End it all. I'm glad he hasn't because that starts playing with your emotions: *Did we do the right thing? The guy's killed himself essentially because of us.* [But] I still feel that guilt. I don't want that guilt. I shouldn't feel guilty. I didn't do anything wrong. I was a kid.'

Indeed, many of the lads – though by no means all – seemed to feel almost guilty that it had come to this; that their actions had resulted in a man in his sixties going to jail. None more so than Doctor Boy.

'It's because I'm a victim,' he explained. 'It's victim psychology. Weirdly, I still feel sorry for him. But that's the victim speaking. That's the GP guy, the Catholic guilt guy, the karma guy. What's done is done,' he added. 'I hope I've helped some other people but whether I've helped myself I'm not sure. Revenge is a dish best served cold. And this has been served very chilly indeed.'

We all walked out of the court into the muggy Manchester air. The other journalists queued up to interview a senior officer from Greater Manchester Police called DCI Chris Bridge. I'd never seen him before; he was asked about his reaction to the case, if he was horrified by the crimes and about the courage of the victims. As he spoke, Charlotte, Jed, Barry and Nicola all walked away in complete anonymity.

After Alan Morris was sentenced, it was a time for statements, soul searching, sympathy and subtly placed reminders of time and place. The Diocese of Shrewsbury, which gave Morris his job at Holy Angels, said, 'The offences against minors committed by Alan Morris when he was a teacher at St Ambrose College are a source of great sadness and regret... Our thoughts and our prayers are very much with the innocent victims of the abuse carried out by Morris. We would like to assure them that the Diocese of Shrewsbury is totally committed to ensuring the safety of all children and vulnerable people in our parishes, schools and institutions. When, in autumn 2012, the diocese was alerted to allegations against Morris, it reported them to the police without hesitation and, acting fully in accordance with nationally agreed and stringent safeguarding guidelines of the Catholic Church, immediately withdrew Mr Morris from active ministry as a deacon. None of the offences was committed within the context of that ministry.'

I spent three months trying to get the diocese to speak to me about the case. They initially seemed keen to help but that slowly ebbed away, until I was told that they weren't willing to be interviewed but that I could submit half a dozen written questions.

Reluctantly, I did. I asked about their child-protection officer's meeting with Doctor Boy at the start of the investigation. I wanted to know what the diocese did when Ground Zero Boy complained about Morris in 2001 and asked about the assurances they had given to parishioners after Morris was arrested in 2012, given that he had access to children at Holy Angels.

The main thing I wanted to know was this: 'The trial heard repeated concerns, complaints and warnings regarding Morris dating back to 1972. He was warned by the school governors and complaints were made by parents about the sexualised nature of his use of corporal punishment – it was, according to police, abuse on an "industrial scale". What checks were made before Morris was given the job at Holy Angels?'

Carol Lawrence – financial secretary of the Diocese of Shrewsbury – emailed me on 11 December 2014 and told me that, having taking legal advice, they would not be able to assist me any further on this matter. She also wished me a merry Christmas.

The Old Boys' Association – who had taken a neutral stance throughout the case and had been advised not to speak publicly about it – also released a statement after Morris was sentenced:

St Ambrose Old Boys Association wishes to acknowledge the prolonged distress and suffering caused to those fellow pupils... who were victims of former teacher Alan Morris between 1972 and 1990. At the same time we recognise the strength, courage and persistence shown by those individuals who came forward to the police and child protection authorities to take the necessary steps which led to his conviction and sentencing. Our prayers are with you.

Ex-pupils like Tim Gresty – who'd started at the school in 1953 – had followed the case throughout and were horrified by what they saw on TV and read in their newspapers about the school they once cherished.

'When I look back on it, there was good clay at the school to make some good pots,' Gresty told me. 'Perhaps there was very good clay among the people who were picked on and damaged by the horrors that were imposed at St Ambrose and that were accelerated by Alan Morris and others like him. I don't think that St Ambrose is alone, I don't think it was unique, I don't think Alan Morris was necessarily unique within St Ambrose but he's the one that's in the spotlight. I'm still trying to find out why he was considered normal by those who knew it was going on, by those that delegated the application of these punishments to him and those who since have supported or even covered up such behaviour. I regard that as horrid. *Horrid.* My mother put her life and soul into raising funds for the school and getting it up to the standard and the status it achieved pre-Alan Morris and the trial. I'm horrified that her association with the school has been lessened by such awful, awful events. I used to drive past the school and the Holy Angels Church with pride. I can't now. That's nothing compared to the damage done to the kids that were affected by the horrors of St Ambrose.

'The fact that Alan Morris transferred to the Holy Angels in a position of responsibility, when it was known there were allegations... I find that a bit chilling.

'I am very proud of what the school provided to me and to many friends I have. I also know there are other people – MPs, businessmen, whatever – who went through St Ambrose and gained. I also recognise it screwed up the lives of a lot of people. Forgiving is very difficult. I'm a practising Christian and I live in a world where I'm told there can be forgiveness. I find it difficult to forgive such behaviour and I find it doubly difficult to forgive the fact that such behaviour was allowed to continue.'

The school itself refused all requests to be interviewed about the investigation or the verdict – not just mine, everyone else's too. The current headmaster Michael Thompson said he'd have to 'politely decline' my offer for him to have his say and referred me to a statement given by the governing body of the school. For the record, here it is:

St. Ambrose College would like to express its sincere regret for any harm suffered by the individuals concerned. Those working in education are particularly appalled by any form of child abuse and we find it abhorrent that Mr Morris has been found to have betrayed the trust and responsibility that had been placed in him as a teacher.

The incidents occurred many years ago and we would like to reassure parents, guardians and relatives that we have contemporary child safety policies in place and ensuring our pupils enjoy a happy and secure childhood and adolescence is our absolute priority. St Ambrose College cooperated fully with the police investigation and provided as much assistance as possible and we would like to thank the police for their diligent and exhaustive approach.

One ex-pupil – I've referred to him as Business Boy – was so incensed by what he felt was a dismissive attitude that he'd put aside a huge amount of money to bring the school to account.

He also contacted them by email, describing his disquiet about events. Business Boy, now based overseas, wanted to know why people had 'covered' for a 'proven criminal' like Alan Morris, why complaints he'd made about Morris in the past were not dealt with and why the school made no apparent objection to Morris's move to Holy Angels.

'I find it amazing that every teacher knew what was going on and the fact the school sanctioned his move to the church next door is incredible,' he wrote. 'The statement issued from the school this week is pitiful, demeaning to all those who suffered. There are so many more people to come forward. In the meanwhile I believe you are still employing very questionable people.'

'This stuff has been on my mind for years and years and years,' he told me. 'They knew what was going on. They're adults. I've got a pretty big company and I know if someone's doing something wrong after about five minutes. For them not to know, to not come forward and to be cowards is just wrong.'

He says he got no reply from St Ambrose but also sent a copy to the police, who took a keen interest in what Business Boy had to say. On Monday, 29 September 2014 the police met with Trafford Council's Safeguarding Children Unit. (St Ambrose, despite the fact it may see itself as a Cheshire kind of school, is actually in the borough of Trafford, Greater Manchester.)

Business Boy's letter was discussed and two members of staff were suspended from St Ambrose. The police assumed that the school would make some sort of statement to reassure parents. There was silence for five weeks until, frustrated by the lack of acknowledgement by St Ambrose, I leaked news of the suspensions to the press to force the school's hand. It felt like the culture of silence hadn't changed much after all these years.

St Ambrose then released a statement:

Following allegations from a former pupil that two members of staff may have been aware of Alan Morris's activities, on the advice of the police and local authority the school has suspended those two members of staff pending an independent inquiry.

The case of the two teachers and what they (or anyone else) knew about Morris was referred to the Catholic Safeguarding Advisory Service, which advises the Catholic Church on child-protection issues. Probably aware that it might look like a case of the Church investigating itself, the service asked an independent investigation firm from outside the area to carry out the work. Five months after the teachers were suspended, I was contacted by the investigator to ask if I'd give evidence.

At the end of February 2015, I went to Salford Cathedral and told them what I knew, including that, although there had been two teachers suspended, I'd found a third who had also been at the school during Alan Morris's time and who the investigators weren't aware of.

I also took the opportunity to ask the person carrying out the probe – 'Investigator Woman' – how it was going. Progress was slow, she admitted. 'You're not going to get a religious order or a diocese falling over themselves to give you information. Often that's information that's adverse to them, although they are obliged to be open and honest. It's not that the diocese is being obstructive but the co-ordinator is overwhelmed by the amount of work she has to do. The police have been helpful but you've pointed me towards things I didn't even know existed. I took a risk with contacting you because you're a journalist. You know more about this than anybody else, so it's worth that risk. I'm closer to getting to the bottom of this, having spoken to you. I've got some leads I can follow. Whether it's possible to get right to the bottom of the truth in something that happened so long away, where a lot of the players are dead, I don't know. I'm not going to be interviewing Alan Morris but would he tell me anything anyway? I'll be able to put together a report that gives people more information than they've already got. Not as much information as you've got though!'

Getting to the truth – it's never easy. When the St Ambrose teachers were suspended, I'd asked the school's headmaster, Michael Thompson, if he'd like to take the opportunity to speak to me and clear the air. Once again, he emailed me and very politely declined but wished me well in my work. I replied with three words: *Vitam Impendere Vero*. It was slightly vulgar of me, I know, but it was hard to resist...

Eleven days later, Michael Thompson emailed parents and told them he had decided to retire as headmaster of the school. 'I have been headmaster of St Ambrose College for fifteen years and it is time now to hand over the reins to a new head to lead the school into the next phase of its development,' his email read. 'I am incredibly proud of the college, the governors, the staff and – of course – the boys. I am also incredibly proud of what we have all achieved over those years. There have been so many changes – I hope most for the better!'

CHAPTER THIRTEEN

STAY DOG

Ever since I left St Ambrose College in 1981, I had a little ritual I carried out every time I drove past the school. It's a very 1970s thing – I flicked the Vs, an old-fashioned two-fingered salute to the school I hated so much. I'd been doing it for more than thirty years.

I live elsewhere now but I pass through Hale Barns regularly to visit my parents, who still live in the same terraced house where I grew up. One of my younger children once spotted me giving my salute from the backseat so, since then, I did it below their line of sight.

Since the end of the trial, I've stopped doing it altogether. That's progress, I suppose. And progress is vital if we're going to cut away the ties that bind so many of the lads to the past. The St Ambrose of the Alan Morris years is nearly all gone. The classrooms, chemistry lab and Dark Room have all been bulldozed. Woodeaves is still there – which must send a chill through those who encountered Brother Baylor and his mattress – but the rest is no more.

For many of the lads, it's the school that's as much to blame as Morris himself for what happened. And that sense of injustice can't be removed with a wrecking ball and a JCB.

'It's great that Alan Morris is in prison now,' says Andy Rothwell, who gave evidence in the first trial. 'I feel that some justice has been served. What I'm pissed off about is that other teachers used to run to him... they knew this was going on. No one was there to protect us. I'd say 80 per cent of them were rotten. They knew what was happening, they knew he was horrible and yet they never stood up to him. No one ever stood up to him. I'd like to confront them and say, "You knew what was going on. Why didn't you do something?" I'd love to do that.'

'It was a good idea to get him locked up,' says Derek Scanlan, who I spoke to on a flying visit to Manchester on his way back to the Outer Hebrides. 'Putting these guys away makes people realise what can happen if people aren't supervised properly with children. It's got to be a good thing. But the culture of the school has never been addressed. They've put one guy away. They all probably think they're safe now. He was being fed victims. At best, other teachers were turning a blind eye and, at worst, they were encouraging it. I would appreciate a proper apology from the board of the school. Morris was seriously evil. He took the abuse to another level: the sexual aspect. There were plenty of other abusive, really violent teachers at that school and that needs to be addressed as well. I hope they get round to that.'

Derek was with his partner, Elsie Mitchell, the day we spoke. She sat quietly as I started to ask Derek a few questions. My first one was, I thought, relatively benign: 'What were your first impressions of the school when you were eleven?'

Derek's eyes immediately sheened over with tears.

'It's been very difficult for Derek,' Elsie told me. 'Because Morris didn't plead guilty, it meant everyone had to drag their minds back to these incidents. It's been an upsetting thing. I didn't know about the sexual abuse aspect until last year. When he talked about his schooling – I went to a rough comprehensive and corporal punishment had just been banned in Scotland – the stories they came out with about teachers hitting them with anything to hand, the violence of it all, I was incredulous. It was like something from the 1940s. They'd treat it like it was funny and laugh it off. It's like they want to ignore what they did to those children. If they wanted to prove that they don't have any of that kind of culture in the school anymore, they should acknowledge what went on and the impact that's had on people's lives. They don't want to because they want people to keep paying their fees.'

Derek told me he still carried the scars of his schooldays to this day. I thought he was being metaphorical and then he showed me the backs of his fingers.

'I was fourteen or fifteen and another boy attacked me with a scalpel,' he said, showing me the scars. 'He tried to go for my face but I put my hand up. It just seemed normal.'

People now know that things were far from normal at

233

St Ambrose. The news of the case went far and wide. Scott Morgan outed himself as a victim and gave a syndicated interview about his time at the school and the near-daily abuse he received from Alan Morris. People might think he got a tidy wedge for his story. They'd be wrong.

'It was a couple of hundred quid,' he told me. 'I shouldn't have done it. I thought it might be a release to get it out. It made no difference. It's all forgotten. I got a few people saying well done for doing it and that kind of made it worthwhile. A lot of people who weren't involved in the trial have contacted me since – they're angry it took so long. I tried to leave it behind twenty-odd years ago. I was kind of forced into seeing Nicola [Graham] and Barry [Conway]. I just really want to forget it. What happened happened. You've just got to live it.'

Those hoping for a big payout for compensations claims are likely to be similarly disappointed. In this country, compensation is awarded by judges, not juries – and judges aren't noted for their generosity. But Richard Scorer from Slater & Gordon believes that launching such claims against institutions like the Church are a vital part of the campaign to bring them to account.

'Compensation actions have been an important part of changing the way the Catholic Church has had to respond to this,' he told me. 'In America, where amounts are awarded by juries, they've had to deal with child abuse because the alternative is bankruptcy. Here, the awards are lower, the financial impact isn't as great, but it's still an impact and it still forces them to deal with it. It forces them to confront things that otherwise they wouldn't want to face up to.

Within the law, there are only a limited number of ways we can get accountability: one is prosecution, the other is to bring claims of financial compensation. All we have is jail and compensation. And taking compensation action against an organisation improves child protection for the future.'

By summer 2015 the St Ambrose compensation claims began to be dealt with by the firm acting on behalf of the Christian Brothers, Hill Dickinson, based in Liverpool. Some lads settled, others didn't. Some lads bypassed the likes of Slater & Gordon and dealt directly with the 'opposition', claiming it resulted in higher payouts. I'd only signed up so that Slater & Gordon would have to talk to me about the progress of the compensation action. I was offered three grand – £2,250 when the costs were subtracted. I was advised to accept it. I took the advice and took the money – but despite the fact I could have really used it... I didn't want it. I divvied it up and gave it to members of my family.

I had hundreds of messages via social media and email once the TV piece about the trial was aired. I even received one on Christmas Day. I read many long and painful accounts from ex-pupils who hadn't felt able to come forward to police. Many of them started with the same words: 'I don't know if you remember me...'

We're like a family now, these lads and I. A big, ugly, messed-up, middle-aged family but a family nonetheless. I won't use the word 'dysfunctional' to describe them because, considering what many have been through, the lads function pretty well. I also try to avoid the word 'victim'.

I'm no one's victim, thank you very much, and neither are any of the lads I've met during the case. Ex-pupil Andy Rothwell put it best: 'I wouldn't class myself as a victim,' he told me. 'A victim is someone who shies away and doesn't want to say anything.'

That's one of the positives that came out of this story: the lads didn't shy away. They stood up and were counted. And that's had a knock-on effect, too. As a direct result of the St Ambrose case, former pupils at nearby Altrincham Grammar School came forward to talk to police based in the same unit as the Alan Morris investigation. They wanted to talk to officers about one of their ex-teachers: Fred Talbot. The TV weatherman is now in jail after being sentenced to five years – he was found guilty of indecently assaulting two teenage boys in the 1970s.

For some of the St Ambrose lads, the whole thing has laid a few ghosts to rest; for others, it's a work in progress. The police in this country may now be better equipped to respond to allegations of historic abuse but they'd be sitting on their hands doing nothing if it wasn't for 'victims' coming forward. It may not always end in a prosecution or a prison sentence but it might help make them feel better about what happened to themselves.

But, as we saw from some of the lads' reactions after Alan Morris was sentenced, even that's not guaranteed. Making that call, giving evidence, going to court – none of these things are easy. So should people come forward? It seems sensible to ask those we've met along the way.

'Definitely worth coming forward,' says Andy Rothwell,

'otherwise these people will carry on existing and get more confident. That's the last thing I'd want. I don't think we can stamp it out forever but we've got more of a chance if people out there come forward.'

'It was necessary,' confirms Paul Wills. 'There's always a cost though. The hard part was living in the past. No one should have to do that. School should have been something you passed through with a few fond memories, a few unpleasant ones. It shouldn't have this kind of effect. [But] times have changed. The police are more receptive now – they are bending over backwards these days because they've missed so many things in the past. My dealings with Barry and Nicola were incredibly professional, without being cold. The police have heard it all before. They're not weary of it but they recognise the truth when they hear it. But a lot of people really don't want to know. I don't know if they're embarrassed or they think it's embarrassing for me. I'm upfront. But some people don't want to know. Even my mum doesn't want to know.'

'I would say to people that this is a golden period in that we can go to the police and be taken seriously,' affirms Nervous Boy. 'There is now somewhere to go to, which we never had. The police were very good with me and dealt with it very well. I know there's some good police but they have had a bad reputation in the past, so I've not been their biggest supporters but I've been impressed by their professionalism – in regards to this case, anyway. I do believe you will be treated seriously and properly.'

'Nobody should ever have to suffer in silence,' asserts Mike Bishop, 'but, in my mind's eye, I've done the right thing – if there is somebody above us, I'll be judged when I'm judged. Justice needed to be done, whichever way you slice it, and I think it has been done. It's not easy to deal with, no matter how simple some might make it look. But, if you can deal with the possible ramifications, if you can deal with the possible problems, if you can deal with the potential invasion of your privacy – which we've all had, to be fair – you've got to tell your story. I take a lot of personal pride in what I've done. I'm thankful to whoever stuck his head above the parapet initially and said, "This story needs to be told." We wouldn't be here now if that hadn't happened.'

That person was Ground Zero Boy. We've reconnected now; we've been out and about together and he's been to my house and met my family. We are friends again. It's been one of the strangest, yet most satisfying aspects of this whole business. When I interviewed him, I said at the start, 'Bet you didn't think we'd be doing *this* thirty-five years down the line.' He's the one who started this whole thing – he opened up the box in 2001 – so I asked him why he'd done it:

Ground Zero: There was a dawning sense of just how dangerous Alan Morris was and, when I discovered he was in charge of groups of children, there was only one possibility. I had to tell somebody so they could make him stop.
But they didn't believe you...
They did believe me. But, unfortunately, there was no corroboration of that evidence, so he was allowed to go free.

How did you feel? Because I knew. You knew. We all knew...

I felt like absolutely nothing had changed. And that wasn't good enough.

You had to sit it out for years. What changed?

They said plenty of other people had now come forward and would I come forward again as well?

Should people who've experienced things like this come forward? What's your advice to them?

You're not supposed to be going through stuff like this when you're young. Anyone who's doing that to you will get locked up. I would say... tell somebody. Just tell somebody. One person, if that's all you can do. But tell somebody and then run away and shout *so loud*. Don't go back to that school or that youth club or wherever it is. Shout from the rooftops about what's happening to you and don't go back. Stand your ground and say, "No." Believe me, when you've got the authorities – genuinely good people – on your side, it's a very powerful feeling to have. My experience of that is of being treated very respectfully and gently. I highly recommend you don't shy away from it. I came forward because I knew he had to be stopped. Because of that, a man is now in jail.

We used to joke about it when we were kids. What about now? Have you drawn a line under this?

I drew my line years ago. I probably drew my line when I was still at school. I came forward for other people – not for retribution or revenge but because I knew he had to be stopped. I used to laugh about it when I was school.

That was how we managed it. But make no mistake about it, I did something that put a guy in jail. It took quite a lot of years to do that. So my advice is... keep smiling. And do the right thing.

It all seems like a long time ago now, doesn't it?
Not long enough...

The other person who the lads should be most grateful towards is Doctor Boy. He has been, by his own admission, a reluctant witness to all of this. 'Doing the right thing' is rarely played out in black and white and, if you ever need an example of that, try the complex triangle the case created between Alan Morris, Doctor Boy and Doctor Dad.

This whole experience has been hard for dad and boy alike. I wondered how their relationship was now. Doctor Dad had taken the decision all those years back not to complain about Alan Morris masturbating in front of his teenage son. I asked Doctor Boy if, since the trial had finished, his dad had apologised to him.

'No, he didn't. My dad's not a great apologiser. I don't hold it against him. I think [my parents] made a funny decision at the time. But, as DC Barry Conway pointed out, if the decision had been made at the time, nothing probably would have happened. It would be another pupil who'd made a nasty, unfounded complaint against a master. It would have been him or me and it would have been swept under the carpet. It needed the weight of historical evidence – multiple complaints across multiple years – to bring that to a jury.'

I put the same question to Doctor Dad: did you apologise?

'No. I say that very thoughtfully. "If only" is a dreadful expression. Why would I say sorry for something that was, arguably, the best decision at the time? We talked together. We drew certain conclusions at the time and came to decisions – that was then and those decisions were made in the context of that particular situation. You can't look at it now [and ask], should you have made a different decision? It's almost an irrelevant question. It can't happen. I couldn't make that decision in the context of information I didn't have and changed attitudes in the future.

'I was talking to one of my son's friends and they said, "Have you got no loyalty?" I said, "If you mean, shall I support him when I think he's done something wrong, then no. If that's how you judge loyalty, then I'm totally disloyal." He doesn't deserve my support just because he's my son. That's not a sensible way to go about it.'

Like I say, complex dynamics.

At the risk of sounding a little touchy-feely – we ex-Ambrose lads don't really do that – I've met some amazing men during this process. Some great women too but this is very much a tale of boys and men. And these men deserve our thanks for being so open.

Since the trial finished, another process has been taking place: difficult conversations between middle-aged men and their parents. Many of the lads never mentioned what happened at school until after they'd told the police.

'The hardest bit for me was [that], up until 2012, my dad had known nothing and I'm very close to my dad,' Mike Bishop told me. 'Mum and Dad divorced when I was sixteen, seventeen. But Mum didn't tell him either. So he was angry at her for not telling him, he was upset, disappointed with me for not saying anything.'

I asked my own mum how she felt. It must have taken a lot of courage for her to go up to the school in the early 1970s and ask about getting me a place there. St Ambrose was intimidating. It made kids feel small – and some adults too.

'It was a mixture of things,' she told me after the trial was over. 'Disgust: that I didn't know what had gone on. Annoyed: to think I put you in their care, thinking I was doing the best for you and it was the opposite. I feel hate. It's wrong – it still goes on but it shouldn't. It will still go on unless people talk about it. They don't because they think people won't believe them. People have only started speaking out since Jimmy Savile and Rolf Harris. There isn't a day goes by without another case cropping up. Why didn't we know about it? Why has it been locked away? People higher up than me and your dad should have spoken out and asked more questions.'

That's a very upsetting phrase: 'people higher up'. The school made working-class parents feel they should know their place and keep their opinions to themselves; they should just be grateful they'd been allowed in and shut up. That's how Morris remained unchallenged for so long.

I have a very telling memory from my childhood: if I'd been off ill and needed to take a letter explaining my absence to school, I'd write out the letter myself. My mum or dad then used to copy it out in their own handwriting. They didn't want the school looking down on them because of their spelling or grammar. That still makes me angry.

For me, my big worry was how my parents would react after the TV report went out. I always ring my dad at 10am on a Sunday morning; the Sunday after the trial finished, I rang him as usual but I was fearful about what he'd say.

It had been on the telly and the reaction had been huge, with hundreds of messages on email and social media. That's all well and good but what would Dad think? I was worried he'd be angry with me for washing so much dirty linen in public. He certainly wasn't someone to ladle out compliments – I don't recall him ever praising me.

(Apparently, it was his way of stopping me getting 'big headed'. Well, there's one tactic that never worked...)

When he picked up the phone, he didn't say, 'Hello.' He said, 'I suppose you'll be getting an OBE now? Well done... proud of you... that took some guts.'

Wow.

In all, seventy-five lads came forward to help police investigate what happened at St Ambrose College in Hale Barns – followed by another thirty after Alan Morris went to jail. Some found comfort in his sentencing; others, like Simon O'Brien, who was so badly treated throughout his school life, are still looking for it. But he's getting there.

'Where I live there's some beautiful countryside,' he told me. 'I walk my dog and, when I get to the far field, where there's no one else around, I have just been overtaken with grief. I have to take water with me because I can't breathe. It takes me the length of the field to break down. I'm safe, I can unload. That's where I cry. I now walk that field and it's gone. It's out. The human psyche is designed to purge it. It's like a cold or the flu: your body gets rid of it. I caught it just in time. I had medical support from my bosses, [so] I'd say get it out in the open. Find someone you trust. Find neutral ground. Let the professionals treat you. I'd have run a mile from that a few years ago [but] give in to it. The journey will be rough but, when you poke out of the other side, my God... I feel like the world has been lifted from my shoulders. It's like a poison that has to come out.'

Talking to the police, however reluctantly, is probably the only way such a process can start. 'It's a personal decision and I would never criticise anyone who decides not to come forward,' says DC Barry Conway, 'but we'll support a hundred per cent the people who do and I think that's the way it should be. It is a difficult decision to stand in front of a court with twelve strangers on the jury, barristers, judges and all that formality, and to go through a sensitive personal experience. It must be one of the most mind-blowing things you'll ever do and I will never underestimate that.

'The system is as good now as it's ever been and I've been in the police for twenty-three years. But there's always room for improvement and the other thing is not to build people's hopes up as well. We can't give assurances; we can't guarantee that the offender is going to be charged or go to court. We definitely can't guarantee there's going to be a conviction because the two trials have shown how different it can be for the same case. But I have the utmost respect for everyone who came forward in this trial and gave evidence. For putting themselves through that, to stick their head above the parapet, all credit to them. It's not my case or Mr Pidd's case or Nicola's case...

it's their case. I just put the paperwork together. It's all about them – that's why you want to win.'

The sheer volume of testimony the St Ambrose case generated – almost a hundred lads have come forward and that number is still rising – made it unique for Greater Manchester Police. 'It's the biggest job of its kind in Manchester,' says DI Jed Pidd. 'So many complainants, so many witnesses. You'll never have heard of a trial split into three because of the numbers before. Call it providence, call it what you will, but we got the right officers to do the right job at the right time. So, yes, it was hugely and massively successful; a job really well done by DCs Nicola Graham and Barry Conway.'

Nicola and Barry 'split up' after the case was over and moved onto other investigations. They are still in touch with many of the lads they dealt with over the two years – it doesn't just end when the shutters come down at court. People still have questions, concerns and a need to talk.

Nicola Graham is now heading for retirement – she has a countdown-clock app on her phone, telling her how long it is until the exact moment arrives. 'I've peaked, haven't I?' she says when I ask her about the Morris case. 'You can't get better than that investigation. It has been very, very tiring. I still have a few big cases on the go. My specialist subject is "historics" – I like them, so I have enough to keep me going but, yes, it was good, it was worth it. It was worth it because it was a community thing; being local made it a lot more personal. I didn't know any of the Ambrose victims at all but they're my peer group, a lot of them, so that was good – a job well done.'

So we know where Alan Morris did it; we know how he did

it and we know some of the people he did it to. What we can only guess at is *why* he did it. What was it inside Morris that made him want to beat, indecently touch and voyeuristically film young boys in his care? Why did he carry on when so many people knew what he was doing? What made him think he would never be challenged or caught?

There's only one person who can provide some of the answers here, so it seemed sensible to ask his opinion. I wrote to him care of Her Majesty's Prison Manchester, known locally as the Strangeways Hotel:

Dear Alan

My name is David Nolan, I'm an ex-pupil of yours, but you will probably remember me slightly more easily as the person who was shouting the St Ambrose school motto outside court during your trial.

First, I am writing to see how you are. It's a genuine query – many of the people involved in the investigation felt a sadness that things had come to this, despite being genuinely damaged by their experiences.

I was due to give evidence in the second trial but withdrew it to follow the process as a journalist – I've been a journalist for thirty-three years, ever since Mr Hibbert gave me the details of a job on a magazine that was available in Altrincham when I was sixteen. I've worked in newspapers, radio and television. I've done pretty well, considering.

I am also an author – I've had nine books published and my tenth will be about St Ambrose. The point of this book will be to explain the process and reality of an historic investigation.

With that in mind, I wanted to ask you about your feelings now towards your ex-pupils and the police and if you felt there were events in your past that had contributed to the position you now find yourself in. I appreciate your childhood was not easy – I believe you lost your father at an early age – were there factors that you didn't reveal that could have been part of the picture?

I have enclosed a SAE if you feel you wish to have your say. I would publish it verbatim.

Yours faithfully

David Nolan

I never did get a reply.

During the two years I was involved in the Alan Morris case, virtually every day brought me back to the words, 'Oh God, *I remember that*': a teacher, an event, a piece of horror or humour that had slipped my mind until one of the lads snapped it back. I'd completely forgotten about Morris's club foot until I saw him at court on the first day of the trial. I couldn't recall the name of the elderly woman who beat the pupils with her walking stick until Paul Quinn reminded me it was Mrs James. It was Ground Zero who reminded me of the boy who had to be hosed down after an attack of diarrhoea during games. He also reminded me the poor lad was nicknamed Pip for the rest of his school life: it stood for 'Poos in Pants'. Kids really can be cruel...

The odd rituals and sayings of the playground came flooding back to me. You may leave school but it never really leaves you. One piece of playground patois was 'stay dog', as trial one 'victim' Paul Wills reminded me.

In St Ambrose-speak, stay dog meant be alert; look out for those around you; keep your head down but your eyes and ears open; make sure your mates are OK. If there's one piece of advice I can give after all this, one thing I've learned through the process, it's... stay dog.

Don't run your life as if there are paedophiles around every corner because that doesn't benefit anyone, least of all your children. But be alert – stay dog – and, if needs be, speak out. Because silence is the great enabler in this situation and silence can be deafening, whether it relates to something from last week or the 1970s.

Don't listen to those people who say, 'It doesn't matter, it's all in the past.' They're wrong.

'It's not in the past – it's with those victims every day,' says Charlotte Crangle of the CPS. 'It'll never be in the past for them until they've confronted it and confronted the person responsible. It's had a profound impact on the rest of their lives, so just because it happened twenty, thirty years ago doesn't make it any less wrong. You often find with victims in cases like this [that] it's burned on their memories; they've relived it time and time again. The people who regret coming forward are very rare in my experience – even if the case has ended up with an acquittal. Some say they wish they'd done it years ago. Once they get to court, they realise things aren't as intimidating as they think. It's the anticipation and the waiting that's worse than giving evidence. Once they start telling their story, they forget the nerves and the tensions and they feel like a weight has been lifted from their shoulders once they've given their account. Always come forward.'

So, if you've got something to say, stand up and say it. It's down to us. Because, as it stands, you can't rely on institutions – *any* institutions – to necessarily do what's best for our children. Why? Because the law doesn't insist that they do so. Hard as it may be to believe, it's not illegal to turn a blind eye.

'If you're working with children, there is no criminal law that says, if you know about abuse or suspect it, you've got to report it – and if you don't report it, you're committing a criminal offence,' says Richard Scorer of Slater & Gordon. 'If you look back over the last thirty years, there are so many cases where, if there had been that legal obligation, the abuse would have been reported, the abuser would have been stopped in their tracks at that point. We need a mandatory reporting law so there's a legal obligation on people in these institutions to report suspicions of abuse. That's what we're arguing for. Most countries have one: Canada, Australia, many states in the US do. We are behind the curve internationally. We absolutely need that if we're going to avoid this kind of thing in the future – or, at least, stop it much sooner. If someone was abusing kids over a twenty-year period and there were suspicions from the start, so much of that abuse could have been stopped if there was a legal obligation to report it and they knew they could go to jail if they didn't. Think of what could have been prevented.'

Astonishing as it seems, it's always been perfectly legal

to look the other way when a child is being abused in this country, even if it's your job to care for children. Campaigners want mandatory reporting laws to be brought in to force the hands of those who witness abuse but don't report it. David Cameron says child abuse should be treated as a 'national threat' equivalent to terrorism or organised crime and wants to extend the offence of 'wilful neglect' that covers anyone vulnerable, from the elderly to children. That could see teachers, social workers and other public officials jailed for up to five years if they look the other way.

Campaigners say this doesn't go far enough but the devil – if you'll forgive the expression – will be in the detail.

In the meantime, it looks like it's down to the likes of the St Ambrose lads to speak out and get things done. And it's down to the rest of you to stay dog until the law tips in favour of children and away from all those members of staff at schools whose corridors are stalked by the likes of Alan Morris, yet who say nothing. Shame on them...

So stay dog but, if needs be, speak out. If we don't, the guilty go unpunished, the truth goes untold and the Alan Morrises of this world go un-shamed. And that's unacceptable.

'Child abuse is about the theft of innocence,' says DI Jed Pidd. 'If you steal a car, you might be able to give that back. It's not the same with child abuse – you can't give innocence back. That's why it's so important to take the perpetrators through the criminal justice system, because they have to repay society and the victims. They have to repay that theft of innocence.'